$6.95

"~~generation gaps~~" rather than a violent
ting structures—and
al to youth, parents,
ness community, and

The Ripon Society
INSTEAD OF REVOLUTION

Introduction by
Senator Howard H. Baker, Jr.

ety is an organization
als, thoroughly com-
publican party—and
ntributors to INSTEAD
have impressive ex-
rnment, universities,
include a high-rank-
of Labor official, a
e, a White House Fel-
nking aides in the
ealth, Education, and
r staffer on the White
airs Council, a free-
ents of law, business,
nce, and a rock-music
contributes to under-
rs.

Is it necessary to destroy our present
economic and political systems to in-
sure a brighter future? "No!" says The
Ripon Society, a group of young, progressive Republicans working to bring
about change.

INSTEAD OF REVOLUTION—an outgrowth of The Ripon Society's Youth
Report, which was presented to President Richard M. Nixon on December
16, 1969—consists of a series of essays
which analyze the discontents of American youth and offer specific proposals
for change. These clear and well-
reasoned programs urge reforms in the
areas of education, labor, business, the
military, ecology, politics, legal rights,
government service, drugs, and inter-
nationalism.

H. Baker, Jr., who has
duction for INSTEAD
was elected in 1966
ublican senator from
dern times. He is one
and most highly re-
of Congress and ac-
embers of The Ripon
White House to meet
Nixon and present the

The members of The Ripon Society
have generated much publicity with
their endorsement of draft reform and
their insistence that Congress lower the
voting age. In addition, they advocate
the legalization of marijuana, the
formation of a national Foundation for
Youth Service, an internationally organized peace corps, and the abolition
of legal discriminations against youth.
INSTEAD OF REVOLUTION is a thoughtful, intelligent discussion of society's

sign by Judith Lerner

rn Books, Inc.
blishers
fth Avenue
New York 10011
ted in U.S.A.

Also by The Ripon Society

BOOKS

Election '64 (1965)

From Disaster to Distinction: The Rebirth of the Republican Party (1966)

Southern Republicanism and the New South (1966)

The Realities of Vietnam (1968)

Who's Who at Convention '68 (1968)

The Lessons of Victory (1969)

PAPERS

"China Policy"

"Multilateral Foreign Aid"

"Negative Income Tax"

"Republican Party Affairs"

"Revenue Sharing"

"Rights of the Mentally Ill"

"Southwestern Military-Industrial Complex"

"Volunteer Army"

Urban position papers

INSTEAD

OF

REVOLUTION

by

The Ripon Society

Introduction by

Senator Howard H. Baker, Jr.

HAWTHORN BOOKS, INC.

PUBLISHERS   NEW YORK

The authors gratefully acknowledge permission to reprint from the following works:

Howl and Other Poems by Allen Ginsberg. Copyright © 1959, 1956, by Allen Ginsberg. Reprinted by permission of City Lights Books.
The Armies of the Night by Norman Mailer. Copyright © 1968 by Norman Mailer. Reprinted by permission of The World Publishing Company.

ACKNOWLEDGMENTS

This book is an outgrowth and adaptation of The Ripon Society's youth report of September, 1969, which was edited by Bruce K. Chapman with the assistance of Robert Davidson, Frank D. Raines, Christopher Beal, Bink Shorts, William J. Kilberg, Geoffrey Keppel, George F. Gilder, Meredith Morris, Robert Burnham, and Reuben S. Brown. It was published in the September, 1969, *Ripon Forum*. On December 16, 1969, Mr. Chapman and other members of The Ripon Society presented the report personally to President Richard M. Nixon at the White House.

The editor of this book wishes to express his deep appreciation to Robert and Wayne Davidson and K. K. Kalba for preparing lengthy memoranda that were most useful in writing the introductory sections of the book. Also helpful in the preparation of the book were the following members of The Ripon Society: Josiah Lee Auspitz, Clair Warren Rodgers, Jr., Mark Bloomfield, Ralph B. Earle, Jr., Howard F. Gillette, Jr., Daniel S. Hirshfield, and John C. Topping, Jr. Others who were instrumental in producing this book included James P. Jordan, of Senator Howard Baker's staff; Sherm Chickering, of *Moderator* magazine; Tony Jones, of *The Chronicle of Higher Education;* and Paul Fargis and Cammy Bain, of Hawthorn Books, Inc. The manuscript was ably typed by Mary Horgan, Hope Fellows, Ellen Kemp, Laura Rosen, and Susan Tharaud.

Except for the editor and those who typed the manuscript, nobody involved in the preparation of this book was compensated financially for his services.

HOWARD L. REITER

CONTENTS

INTRODUCTION

by Senator Howard H. Baker, Jr.

There has been a great deal of attention devoted to generational conflict in America. Some feel that this tension between generations is a constant of any society and that the outpouring of attention devoted to young Americans today by journalists, politicians, academicians, and others is not only unwarranted but undesirable, in that it feeds upon itself, promotes further division, and minimizes those values and aspirations common to the majority of Americans.

While I find some truth in this view, particularly where attention is focused on the more radical elements of the conflict, I nonetheless sense a special urgency in the rift that exists between growing numbers of Americans. Because a great many young Americans—and some who are not so young, but who are sympathetic to them—now question many of the fundamental premises of our society, I see a conflict that goes beyond the need of every individual to establish his own independence. The society is being asked to justify itself—its values, priorities, aspirations, institutions —and its response to this challenge will, in large part, determine its future.

There are aspects of the youth culture of which I cannot approve, neither as an individual nor as a student of social organization. But these antipathies do not limit the importance that I attach to what is taking place; in some ways, they strengthen it. I am not yet prepared to say that 1970 is a critical point in the evolution of the American experience. Each era seems to those who live in it a pivotal time. But it seems clear that in 1970 the manifestations of unrest and alienation are as overt as they have been in our history. And the central role of young people in this disquiet is without any precedent of which I am aware. In June, 1970, a national polling organization reported that student activism was viewed as a more serious national problem than the war in Southeast Asia, inflation, and crime in the streets. The conflict of generations has become the major national concern.

It is important to begin any discussion of this phenomenon with several disclaimers and qualifications. First, we must bear in mind the limitations implicit in any generalization about large numbers of people. All that young Americans have in common are the fact that they are American citizens and the fact that they are younger than older Americans. The commonly accepted dividing line between the young and the old—the age is thirty—is, of course, entirely arbitrary. It is pointless and misleading to assert that anything approaching the totality of Americans under thirty share a common view of the society and their own future in it. And it is true that many Americans over thirty share strikingly similar views as many under thirty.

Second, it is important that we avoid what is called the fallacy of composition: assuming that what is true of a part is necessarily true of the whole. One venal politician is not evidence that all are venal. One tragic assassination is not evidence that the whole society is sick. One incendiary student radical is no indication that all students are mad bombers. There is altogether too much of this kind of murky thinking on the campuses, in the unions, in the government, and in the press. It is enormously destructive because it obviates the need for hard thought about complex problems.

Having noted these qualifications, we can go on to acknowledge the legitimacy of certain generalizations about young Americans today. Every generalization distorts reality because it oversimplifies, but what is gained in the abstraction hopefully outweighs the more subtle distinctions that are sacrificed. It is a fact that there are significant numbers of young people who are increasingly alienated from the values, aspirations, and institutions of American society. What is perhaps most disturbing about this phenomenon is that the middle ground seems to be shrinking. It has been repeatedly observed during campus disorders that the moderate majority of students has been brought from the sidelines into sympathy with the more militant students by what is viewed by the moderates—rightly or wrongly—as intemperate overreaction by campus and civil authorities. The same kind of reaction seems to be widespread throughout the society: Moderates of all ages and persuasions feel increasingly compelled to take sides.

This polarization manifests itself in a broad spectrum of issues not directly related to the particular grievances of the young. Foreign policy, environmental quality, domestic economic policy, budgetary priorities, educational goals—on all these issues the middle ground is diminishing and more and more Americans are tending to identify with a hard-line position at one end of the spectrum or the other.

I can make no secret of the concern this trend causes me. It bears the seeds of a continuing division that wholly ignores the complexity of the issues and the processes of enlightened compromise whereby legitimate differences are effectively resolved. I have long believed that the particular genius of representative democracy and, in our own case, of the two-party system, is that these institutions inhibit the development of rigid and extreme ideological positions. Any widespread and lasting diminution of a moderate majority will present the American people with some very unpleasant choices.

Perhaps the most "vital" thing about the present conflict between growing numbers of young Americans and their elders is that it centers around the fundamental assumptions and values of our society. Serious disagreement about how the goals of society can best be achieved is essentially a question of tactics and can normally be resolved without too much bitterness. But when the goals themselves become matters of dispute, the potential for bitter division exists.

Confidence in the society, its laws, and its institutions has begun to erode for a number of young people, and this problem demands the serious attention of all thoughtful Americans, regardless of age and station. This is true not only because the alienation of youth is a source of concern, but even more so because these disaffected Americans will soon begin to take positions of authority and responsibility in the society.

Social cohesion—whether between two people or among the

people of a nation—can exist only when there is a sharing of fundamental assumptions and values. This does not mean that all of the basic assumptions and values must be shared or that they must be defined in the same way by every citizen. On the contrary, any society can withstand diverse, often widely divergent, viewpoints about basic values and goals. Many people, and I am among them, attach a basic value to this very diversity. But for any social unit to be truly cohesive and satisfying to its members, there must be a basic commitment to the unit itself, and also a shared assumption that individual differences must at times be subordinated to ensure the survival of that unit.

Characteristic of such social organization is a tolerance of the values of others. It must be widely understood that however little they may be shared, the values of other individuals are quite real to them; they may be deeply held convictions. It is a very serious matter for one human being to demand that another reject the values that give his life its meaning. If the concept of morality has any meaning, it has to do with the way we conduct ourselves with relation to one another. I would attach a fairly high moral value to tolerance of the views of others.

On the contrary, "moralism" too is a creed, but its adherents attempt to regulate the morals of others, to insist on how others should live, and think, and behave. I am concerned that there appears to be a growing tendency toward a rigid moralism among both the disaffected young people and those who react against them. Increasing numbers of people seem to be polarizing around the conflict of American generations, digging in their heels, asserting the absolute correctness of their vision of America's future, rejecting out of hand the views of others, and demanding that the society as a whole adopt their view. For example, many young people who opposed the Cambodian military intervention of May and June, 1970, accused the government of not "listening" to them. But what they probably meant was that the government was not doing what they wanted it to do.

Tolerance of the views of others need not lead to any abandonment of efforts to achieve progressive change in society. One of the great strengths of the youth movement is that it has adopted as its ideology those values that have always been the official policy of our nation: justice, equality of opportunity, freedom of expression. That these ideals have not been realized and are often openly abused in practice is a matter of urgency to many of America's young. They find the disparity between promise and practice intolerable, and the fact that many of them are bent to challenging this hypocrisy holds out great promise. How this challenge is made by the young and how it is met by the society as a whole are questions of paramount importance to the future of the country. If the young insist on instant achievement of ideal goals, they will be met with increasing resistance. If society shows itself incapable of any change, the frustration and bitterness of the young will certainly increase.

There have been many analyses of why such vehement dissension has come about at this particular point in our national history. Many have pointed to growing affluence, to expanded higher education, to the civil-rights movement of the early 1960s, to the life and death of John F. Kennedy, to global communications, to the influence of the Depression on the values of the parents of the young, and, of course, to the war in Vietnam. One of the most perceptive chapters in this book presents the thesis that the civil-rights struggle of the early sixties instilled in many young people a sense of institutional hypocrisy, while protest against the war in Vietnam brought them into a direct confrontation with the institutions of government themselves.

Some commentators tend to downgrade the importance of the war in Vietnam as a prime catalyst in the growing disaffection of youth. I disagree. I think it is hard to overemphasize the role that the war has played in forming the outlook of many of our young people. Although I personally find much of the opposition to America's role in the war dangerously narrow and overly emotional, I think that the government must clearly bear a share of the responsibility for the protests that have taken place.

I mentioned earlier that when they complain of not being heard by the government, many young people seem to mean that the government is not doing what they want it to do, immediately and unconditionally terminate American involvement in the war.

There is an aspect of this complaint that I find much more valid, however. I think that from its very inception the war has been inadequately explained to the American people and particularly to the young men who are asked to fight in it. If the government is not prepared to alter its commitment in Southeast Asia, it seems to me incumbent on government officials to acknowledge the legitimacy of the young's concern and to respond to their criticism. There has been a tendency on the part of the government to make the war issue a test of loyalty and patriotism, thus avoiding the necessity of explaining its policies or acknowledging the uncertainty of their ultimate success. Even if the basic policy remains unchanged, I believe, the young would have a greater feeling of being heard on the issue if their objections were met with rational explanations by the government. Such explanations do exist in the minds of those public officials who make and support our policies for Southeast Asia, and the American people should not be judged incapable of comprehending them.

This kind of discourse would be welcome in other areas of our national life where rigid moralistic viewpoints are replacing tolerance. I firmly believe that the institutions of representative government are capable of dealing with and containing the broadest kind of diversity. But the very effectiveness of these institutions lies in their flexibility, in their capacity to accommodate shifting priorities in times of rapid change. If more and more people take increasingly rigid stands on the great issues of our time, the capacity of our institutions to resolve differences will be impaired. In our history as a people only once, during the War Between the States, have we had a nearly fatal failure of our political institutions, and even then the Union was preserved. There is a compelling need today for Americans of all ages and persuasions to work together toward a kind of "militant moderation."

It is out of this need for moderation that I see an important role for the members of The Ripon Society. They are small in number, but they have achieved a remarkable influence in public affairs due to the general excellence of their work. Although a number of its members are substantially to the left of the mainstream of the Republican party, much of the society's effectiveness is attributable to its capacity to serve as a moderating influence. The society is deeply committed to the American political system and has an abiding conviction that *all* Americans can be served by that system.

This book has been written by several young people, some of them members of The Ripon Society. There are parts of it that I find more rewarding than others, and there are a few parts of it that I find quite mistaken, both as to analysis and recommendation. Chapter 2, entitled "Youth Culture," seems to me to suggest the kind of arrogance, intolerance, self-indulgence, and ignorance of history that are the least redeeming characteristics of some of our young people. But taken as a whole I think that this book can make a significant contribution to our understanding of the youth phenomenon and how we might constructively respond to it. If we refuse to come to grips with aspects of our society that we may find disquieting and uncomfortable, we will not be capable of any real growth.

On balance, I find much that is hopeful in young Americans today. Their idealism, their energy, their increasing knowledge, their willingness to make significant personal sacrifices are all essential ingredients for a better world.

INSTEAD OF REVOLUTION

Chapter 1

THE NEW CONSTITUENCY

Who Is Youth?

Why are the American youth of today set apart from their elders in ways that young people of the past were not? What makes today's young different?

We will attempt no final answers, only some plausible guesses. Then, in later pages, we will outline some of the specific problems and grievances of young people and suggest ways in which the institutions of society can respond constructively to them.

Perhaps we can best begin by taking a journey through time, a journey in the life of a young person of today. He is not a hippie, although he does not recoil at the sight of long hair and love beads. He is not a radical, although he may be more liberal and more idealistic than the average older American. He need not be college-educated, although he has more information at his disposal than any previous generation in history.

Let us start with his parents, for we can understand him largely in contrast to them. They were children in the 1920s, but as they entered adolescence the economy of the nation collapsed. They know (as they have often told their children) what it feels like to worry about not having a job, what it is like to cut corners to have enough to eat, what it is like to defer dreams again and again. Their experience of that time is what is called a formative experience—one that comes at a time in life when it has a lasting effect on a person's whole character, on his goals, his needs, his fears. Probably their primary goal was that their own children would never face the deprivation they had suffered. Then, as the parents reached adulthood, a war against foreign aggression had to be

1

fought. Many went to fight it; those at home had to endure sacrifices for the war cause. Again, the universal desire was that their children would never have to defer dreams, to shed blood, because aggression was not halted soon enough.

With the return of peace and economic security, families were reunited and the great "baby boom" occurred. Around this time, the young person whose life we are chronicling was born. His parents, now comfortably middle-class, responding to the newest theories of child raising and reacting against the harsh austerity that marked the Depression and the war years, brought him up in a freer environment than any generation of the past had known. Some would say this indulgence was responsible for a lack of self-restraint and moral rectitude on the part of the child. At any rate, the young person became accustomed to a life where privation was unknown, where the authorities—his parents—were pliant and reasonable, where blind obedience was not expected of him.

In those years, he began the long vigil in front of the picture tube—puppet shows, entertainment extravaganzas, cowboy epics—and he learned what amazing things were possible. Unlike his parents, for whom the movies had been a once-a-week treat, he become used to marvels several hours a day. They became part of his expectations—the theatrical, the fantastic, the up-to-date.

Then he began school, in an era when patriotism was the watchword, and he was taught that the nation stood for liberty and justice for all, and against Communism, which his parents saw as the successor to the Fascist menace. As he grew a little older, politics did not interest him; but he began to respond to the new music —rock and roll—and identify with its themes: teenage romance, school, parental conflict, motorcycle gangs, an occasional macabre ballad to play on his fascination with death. Parents denounced rock as lewd and obscene, and that made it all the more attractive to teenagers, who saw in it a common bond with their peers.

High school was a time when most young people became exposed to what was seen as the great rat race, and the great put-on as well. The student felt the restraints of parents and teachers unduly oppressive, because he was beginning to feel that he could function without them. Every rule had to be justified, and when an angry elder told him to do something "because I said so," his attitude toward all authority became cynical. It was then that his childhood faith in the honesty and good faith of his elders was most severely tried, and he wanted nothing more than parents and teachers who would speak to him with honesty and understanding. Every order, every rule, seemed to emphasize order and stability, at an age when he wanted freedom and action.

Consequently, all pronouncements from above were suspect: Do well, or you won't get into college or get a good job or stay out of the draft. The young person began to doubt some of the values that animated his parents, notably their desire for material comforts. Young people who have had everything find it difficult to understand parents who know what it is like to have done without. The young person wants wheels, but on a motorcycle or a VW; he is not impressed by a Cadillac or a sprawling ranch house. He wants a job, but not a meaningless nine-to-five routine.

And, of course, our high school student by now was well aware of himself as a sexual being. But he found that his desires brought him in conflict with many of the traditional mores. This was nothing new, but in an age when early upbringing encouraged freedom, the new pressures were especially strong and the young person often found parental ideas constricting.

For many, this conflict was resolved in favor of parental values; for others, in favor of an extreme license, but this often brought insecurity. Still others began to search for a moral code that would enable them to seek love unhindered by many of the ethical precepts of the past. Improved birth-control methods, notably the pill, enabled many young couples to explore sex without the necessity of marriage. In this way, they felt, they could have rich and "meaningful" relationships without committing themselves to a lifelong partnership. And many girls felt that at last they had the sexual freedom that boys had enjoyed for so long.

But one's romantic attachments were just one of many problems in late adolescence. The high school student had to begin to make the choices that would affect the rest of his life—college or job, military service, stay at home or move, and so on. In the 1960s this choice was far broader than it had ever been: Colleges were opening their doors and providing financial aid to millions, and the job market was beckoning. Without fear of being closed off from any alternative, a fear his parents had had, the youngster had time to choose his own style of life. If he went on to college, such speculation was not only tolerated but encouraged. And so it is small wonder that this speculation, combined with skepticism about many parental values, led to a fundamental questioning of society's values.

Of course, thinkers have always questioned the values of their society, and many have been at the vanguard of great social upheavals. But never before in history have so many people, encouraged to be free, skeptical about the past, and with ample leisure time, engaged in such hard questioning.

The fact that the culture throws young people together only increases their drive for independent values and life styles. Rock music cannot be underestimated as a cultural norm, for it gives young people of all backgrounds a common language, while shutting out their parents. Indeed, young people do all they can to perpetuate this group identity. One device is slang, a common language shared by all of the young. As soon as one phrase is picked up by parents and the mass media, young people replace it with others; for example, terms like "cool," "hip," and "groovy" are long since obsolete. One reason that young protesters often indulge in obscenity is that obscenity in public is one of the last ways in which language can be used as protest. In a society that protects free speech, obscenity is about the only thing *not* frequently heard.

Another sign of preserving a common identity is the game of trivia, in which young people vie with each other to remember a song, a movie, or a television show from when they were much younger. The purpose of the game is not to stump the other person but to help him remember a shared experience, to create a heritage from earlier moments in a relatively short life.

In these troubled times, it is frequently death that forges a bond among young people. When a young person is killed in a Mississippi swamp for civil rights, in Vietnam because of a war that nobody wanted, or on a campus because law officers fired on a crowd, most young people feel a sense of outrage and loss: One of my own has died, and responsibility rests with older people.

THEMES AND CROSS-CURRENTS

In past generations youthful energy was expended in taming the frontier, in frenetic dances like the Charleston or jitterbug, in campus pranks like panty raids. Likewise, much of the activity of today's generation, from "lewd" dancing to political activism, is only the most recent manifestation of the need of young people to express themselves in strenuous and energetic ways. To many, the ultimate expression is rebellion, in dress, hair styles, music, politics. Young people have always needed to set themselves apart from their elders. They are determined to strike out on their own, to demonstrate that they can manage their lives without help from their parents. Many of the activities of young people most disconcerting to their parents reflect this need. It is not simply a negative, antiparental rebellion, but a positive attempt to break away and live independently. It is a step toward maturity.

And this brings up another important aspect of all young people, their need to carve out their own identity. In our culture most young people are kept from the pressures of making a living until their late teens or early twenties. Thus they have the time to devote much thought and experimentation to their future. They might switch from job to job, from college major to college major, from one boyfriend or girlfriend to another. This experimentation is not a sign of instability; young people insist on exercising their options, constantly exploring to determine what they really want out of life.

The young express a healthy skepticism about what they hear from their elders, which today translates into the cry "Tell it like it is." They feel that they have been deceived by parents, teachers, employers, and military brass, and too often they are right. In fact, this is one of the most positive aspects of the character of youth, the demand for an end to hypocrisy. Those who lament the lack of respect of young people toward our institutions and our leaders would do well to heed this point.

The needs of today's young are the same as the needs of young people of all eras, differing only in the ways in which they are translated into behavior. For one thing, there is the influence of the mass media. This is not the place to speculate, à la McLuhan, about the vast changes in our culture that have been brought about by the media, but we can note several features of special importance to young people. Television news gives us a sense of power—that is, we see events as they occur, and consequently we feel that we can affect them. Hearing about a riot that has already taken place does not affect us in the same way as seeing one in our city as it is taking place; seeing it may cause us to call the mayor to complain, or maybe to go downtown and catch the action. And when the President of the United States can deliver major addresses in our living rooms, we are less awed by our leaders, because we feel closer to them. All these things encourage activism, an attempt to change the course of major events.

But the media have another important function for youth: They create a community among the young people of America. A rock star appears on television and has a nationwide audience; four youths are gunned down on a campus and the next day everyone knows their names. Motion pictures, too, help disseminate the youth culture across the nation and around the world.

Another great change in recent years has been the enormous increase in leisure time. In the past, young people had to begin work as soon as they were able, and had to work long, hard hours. Today not only is one's entrance into the labor market long deferred, but work hours are shorter. This phenomenon cuts across all of society, of course, but it affects youth most of all because it occurs at a time in life when they are going through the identity problems discussed above. Leisure time enables young people to spend more time wrestling with these problems; it also enables the politically inclined to spend hours organizing and acting.

In addition to having abundant leisure time, most young people are relatively comfortable financially. Instead of wondering where the next dollar is coming from, they are giving hard thought to deciding the kind of life they want. Physically, intellectually, and often emotionally, today's young people are maturing faster than older generations did. And to reach maturity without many of the rights and responsibilities of mature people—such as the vote, legal equality, and a voice in the institutions that govern society—creates frustration. This sense of powerlessness is responsible for many of the anxieties of young people and the resulting social tensions. The demand for rights and privileges commensurate with their duties by young people on campuses, in factories, in offices, and in uniform will be a major theme of this book.

Finally, young people are better educated than any generation of the past. The simple fact is, they know more, in the sciences, in social studies, in the humanities. This knowledge only increases the frustration of powerlessness. Furthermore, more and more young people are learning elementary sociology at an early age. They understand how society's institutions—the family, the church, the school—are designed to "socialize" young people—train them to conform to the values and customs of society. A tremendous amount of tension is created because young people realize what is going on. They feel like guinea pigs in an experiment, and when the guinea pig realizes the purpose of the experiment, he is not likely to cooperate It is rather ironic that sociology, the study of society, can result in the weakening of the processes that unite society!

AMERICA AND ITS YOUTH

The most important thing, perhaps, about the new upheaval of young America is that to a great extent it is motivated by ideals that are among the highest of our civilization. What appears to be hedonism may be a sincere attempt to find better ways of relating to other people; what appears to be radicalism may be a striving to improve the nation for the good of everyone; what appears to be incivility may be only a young person's desire to be natural, to seek free self-expression.

The road that the youth culture will take will depend on the reactions of older Americans. If they choose to react with repression and violence, they will succeed only in converting many more young people to extremism, and will escalate the tensions that are already too high. But if they decide to listen to young people, to consider their demands to reform what must be reformed, then they will achieve far more than better relations between the generations. They will combine the best that youth have to offer—imagination, energy, idealism—with the best that adults have to offer—experience, pragmatism, prudence—and produce a better nation and world.

In the pages that follow, we hope to point out just where reforms can and should be made. But, believing that a movement can often best be understood by the words of its more radical members, we would first like to present a striking essay by one such representative of the youth movement which conveys much of what animates our dissatisfied youth.

Chapter 2

YOUTH CULTURE

"They" and Us

Perhaps the most difficult kind of communication is that between two different cultures. American adults shake their heads in bewilderment over long hair, loud music, and other phenomena which make absolutely no sense to them. Because of the magnitude of this task of communication, we are relying on a more personal kind of statement than those which characterize the rest of this book. For this purpose, Keith Maillard has provided a host of insights that require no further introduction.— ED.

THE FIFTIES: BEAT

I read Jack Kerouac's *On the Road* the year I was a sophomore in high school. That was the middle of the fifties: The golfing President was in the White House, Joe McCarthy was reviving the tradition of the Alien and Sedition Acts, the generation then in college was called "silent," and they didn't call us high school kids anything at all. My family worried a lot about "what other people will think." Some things you did, others you didn't; these unwritten laws had been given at some dim time in the past on some middle-class Mount Sinai, and they were not open to question. You *did* get good grades, get along with other people, dress appropriately for whatever occasion, remain, whatever the situation, unfailingly polite. You *didn't* sleep on the floor (I had wanted to at ten or eleven; the idea wasn't violently repressed, merely derided to death), use bad language, raise your voice (even when you were boiling inside), come to dinner without a shirt, put the milk carton on the table (you put a little glass pitcher of milk on the table),

9

forget to change your socks. It was never stated, but it was clear enough: The most important value was maintaining appearances. The teachers at school were in on the plot; in fact, the whole world seemed to be in on the plot. The message from outside, everywhere, was "this is the only conceivable way things could be; this is the only conceivable way a decent person would want to live." The message from inside my head was slightly different. It could be summed up by Guy Debord's motto for the modern cities: "Nothing will ever happen here, and nothing *ever has*." [1]

My parents' generation engaged in an unreflective pursuit of middle-class values: security, upward mobility, acquisition. Jules Henry described them perfectly when he wrote: "Except for professionals and executives most Americans are emotionally involved neither in their occupations (what they do) nor in their job (the place where they do it). What finally relates the average person to life, space, and people is his own personal, intimate economy: his family, house, and car. He has labelled his occupational world 'not involved,' and turned inward upon his own little world of family, hobbies, and living standard." [2] It could hardly have been otherwise in a generation that had survived the Depression and was struggling to make good in a highly advanced, rapidly expanding and automating capitalist society in which workers are as interchangeable as machine parts (and as likely to become obsolescent) and decisions are made by a distant and unintelligible technocracy.

This "turning inward" of Americans to their "own little world of family, hobbies, and living standard" gave rise to another phenomenon which began to flower in the fifties: the child-centered family. As Henry has so carefully documented in his *Culture Against Man,* the American father dropped his role as distant lawgiver and emerged as "the imp of fun" competing with his wife for the affection of his children. Both parents, the father alienated from his work, the mother alienated from the vast desert of boredom that characterized the life of a housewife, turned to their children for comfort and meaning. But behind the benign mask of their "permissiveness" were the murderous games, referred to by R. D. Laing as those "forces of violence called love," [3] of empty people who have lost their selves and seek to find them in their children. As Freud noted, "The 'unduly lenient and indulgent' father fosters the development of an over-strict super-ego because, in the face of the love which is showered on it, the child has no other way of disposing of its aggressiveness than to turn it inwards." [4] The result of this inward-turned aggression is guilt. *My* generation is one that grew up guilty.

Our movie, *Rebel Without a Cause,* is now laughed at and enjoyed as camp art by a new breed of teenagers who have bounded, it seems in a matter of weeks, the painful journey it took us years to complete. But *Rebel* was no laughing matter for us; it crystallized, in stereotypes of comic-book simplicity, the whole messy, nauseating American scene of the fifties: the inward-turned "little world" of the affluent, middle-class family with its voracious emotional vulture-mother and empty pal-father, the ominous totalitarianism of the adolescent peer group. James Dean was the perfect embodiment of our guilty ambivalence: noisy rebellion masking a fragile sensitivity, inarticulate outward toughness masking an inward desolation just a step away from tears. With *Rebel* we mourned the loss of an America we had never known: an America (in the schoolbook-television-Hollywood images) of the placid mother who baked pies and bore children, of the stern father who was "his own man" and who worked at an intelligible trade and beat the kids when they needed it, of clear-cut moral values (good guys and bad guys), of endless opportunity—an America dying of technology. Dean drags his father to his feet and begs him to "be a man"; with Natalie Wood as mommy and Sal Mineo as child, he re-creates the lost family. The movie ends with the hope that *all* lost values will be regained.

But we knew, even as we experienced it, that the hope was in vain. We have spent years trying to build a new identity; the Beats were the beginning. Present in the Beats were the seeds of every tendency (with the exception of that toward the equalization of the sexes) that would flower in the youth culture of the sixties; Jack Kerouac articulated the guilty, sad longing for a simpler, more "real" life that would continue to haunt us: "At lilac evening I walked with every muscle aching among the lights of 27th and Welton in the Denver colored section, wishing I were a Negro, feeling that the best the white world had offered was not enough ecstasy for me, not enough life, joy, kicks, darkness, music, not enough night. . . . I wished I were a Denver Mexican, or even a poor overworked Jap, anything but what I was so drearily, a 'white man' disillusioned."[5] The declaration of war on the "system" was laid down by Ginsberg, who saw "the best minds of my generation destroyed by madness, starving hysterical naked...," asked "What sphinx of cement and aluminum bashed open their skulls and ate up their brains and imagination?" and answered, "Moloch! Solitude! Filth! Ugliness! Ashcans and Unobtainable dollars! . . . Moloch the incomprehensible prison! Moloch the crossbone soulless jailhouse and Congress of sorrows! Moloch whose buildings are judgment! Moloch the vast stone of war! Moloch the stunned governments! Moloch whose mind is pure machinery! Moloch whose blood is running money!"[6] The fascination with the Orient was heralded by Gary Snyder and celebrated in Kerouac's book about him (The Dharma Bums, where I first saw a reference to the I Ching, now so popular that numerous versions are popping up). Of course, all the Beats dug marijuana; and they all consciously employed elements of Dada (with its anti-everything revolt and mockery of the bourgeoisie) and Surrealist art (with its emphasis on the subconscious, dreams, and the transformation of the world through altered states of consciousness).

The mass media reacted to the Beats as they would later react to the youth culture of the next decade, with derision and slogans. As Lawrence Lipton noted in The Holy Barbarians, his excellent (and, unfortunately, largely unread) book on the Beats: " 'Cynical' is a word that the sensation-mongering newspapers and magazine writers like to tag onto their stories about the beat generation. If the beatnik lives in a state of voluntary poverty, he isn't being sincere about it—how can anybody turn down a buck?—so he must be cynical . . . trying to put on a show of superiority by sneering at all the things that make life really worth living and which he secretly yearns for but hasn't got the get-up-and-go to acquire for himself. This is the party line, and you will find some form of it in all the mass circulation magazines and newspapers whenever they refer to the subject."[7]

"Serious" intellectuals objected that Beat writing was not very good ("good" defined as that writing approved of by college English departments) and that Beat thought smacked of anti-intellectualism. There is, of course, an anti-intellectual bias in Beat writing; it is against intelligence staked out into "disciplines" by "specialists" and "experts": intelligence at the service of power. The thread of Blakean anti-intellectualism runs through all the rebellious gestures of youth in the sixties, and "intellectuals" reacted to it with the same gambits employed against the Beats: These young people don't play by the rules (whether the rules of writing, art, "common decency," or politics); they are sick[8] (but not, of course, the society that produced them); they are Nazis or anarchists (or Communists, or dope fiends, or . . . fill in the blank with whatever epithet embodies the worst fears of the commentator's readership).

ROCK

Rock has been the language of youth culture since the mid-fifties and has come so far in that time that it is now an art form as subtle, expressive, and varied as modern jazz, a form more intense and relevant than all modern bourgeois poetry and fiction. We no longer need to apologize for it. Under the twin siccatives of Academia (English departments are frequently the most hopelessly bourgeois compartments of our hopelessly bourgeois universities) and the publishing industry (writing-as-commodity for the bourgeois buyer), "literature" in America since the Beats is stone dead. (Somehow, by some miracle, a few good books manage to sneak through: Joseph Heller's *Catch-22*, Thomas Pynchon's novels, Leonard Cohen's *Beautiful Losers*.) The "art world" is dominated by a clique of the jaded wealthy (and their handmaidens, the "art" dealers) who regard the latest manifestation of action painting, pop, or op on the same level as a haircut by Kenneth or a dress by Courrèges,[9] leaving those artists who prefer to spend their time in other ways than drinking champagne with rich boors to make a living at worst poorly and at best at an honest trade. "Serious" music is a matter for discussion and elucidation by mini-pedants,[10] film-making is in the heavy hands of Hollywood pomposities, dance under the dictatorship of that tyrant of narrow taste, George Balanchine, and should we bother to talk of architecture? Young people in the last ten years have reacted to this total lock-out of creative talent from the Establishment arts by do-it-yourself projects (underground press and films; underground books, often those of the innumerable brilliant and unpublished young poets now working in America; innovative dance as guerrilla theater or in little broke companies; art as self-expression for the enjoyment of friends or as "graphics" in underground papers) or by entering the only money-making field still open to creativity, life, and talent: rock.

Rock is a business, of course, but the rock market is a youth market, and the young have been developing increasingly anti-bourgeois tastes (even such a tailor-made, plastic, designed-to-make-a-buck group as the Monkees has been forced to knock bourgeois values in order to sell, as in "Day Dream Believer") and there is a sufficient market to allow the release, by a major recording studio, of such weirdly offbeat LP's as *The Moray Eels Eat the Holy Modal Rounders*. Once they make it, rock artists are under tremendous pressure, forced to create in an atmosphere that is, to say the least, murderous. The canniest of them (Frank Zappa, the Beatles) have set up their own companies so to have control over their work or have withdrawn into seclusion (Dylan). Others have burned out and have ended up recording mannered, slick junk. But into that strange mixture of rebels and capitalists that make up the rock industry has gone much of the creative talent and genius (for Dylan and the Beatles the word is not too strong) of the youth culture, and out of it has come that culture's profoundest artistic expression.

What can be said of the Beatles, God knows? Nothing definitive in less than a hundred thousand words (a million?). So all I'll attempt here are a few McLuhanesque "probes" toward the meaning of the Beatles for the sixties. In terms of total sound—music, lyrics, electronic effects—undoubtedly the most interesting rock of the decade. Undoubtedly slick (at times obnoxiously slick). Undoubtedly the most popular group with who knows how many million sellers.

The Beatles first hit America as another of those youth fads they like to laugh about in the mass media. "Beatlemania" was the word. Their image was whimsical, sex tuned down and out, androgynous, boyish and at the same time (especially in Paul) girlish (but not the least bit faggotty): the seeds of unisex. And they were the catalyst for the Great Hair Struggle that would make it—almost—to the Supreme Court. Then, among the teeny-bopper love songs began to appear the weird twang of the Orient and . . . social protest. Social protest? Yeah. Nothing issue-bound like early Dylan, nothing the political heavies could organize around, could, you know . . . use. But social protest nonetheless. Songs about the misery of ordinary people, like the ballads about the ubiquitous taxman or the emptiness of the life of everybody's maiden aunt, Eleanor Rigby.

And then: Freak out! The Beatles (with "*Lucy in the Sky with Diamonds*") are telling every teenage kid who has ears to hear that it's cool to drop acid. And they've learned to spin images together in the floating, free-association way your mind works when you're stoned on grass; and just so we'll get it, they're telling us that they'd love to turn us on. The adult world didn't, of course, freak out over *Sgt. Pepper's Lonely Hearts Club Band,* an album which sold over a million copies[11] and brought the dope message to every kid in America, because *Sgt. Pepper,* like most of the music of the counter culture, is in code. At the radio station where I used to work there is a commonly accepted bit of folk lore: You can get away with anything on the air as long as it's *sung.* The adult world, and that includes the FCC, doesn't really listen to music. That's the first part of the code. The second part lies in what you say. You don't come on, with guitar accompaniment, and sing, "We think it's fine to take LSD, yeah, yeah, yeah!" You sing about Lucy in the Sky with Diamonds. No adult will get the message. Some of the kids will get the message and some won't; but the number that will gets bigger and bigger every day. Mommy and Daddy think everything's taken care of by that five-minute TV spot of "your local law enforcement official" stumbling through his lines about the evils of dope, his nervous eyes bouncing along with the teleprompter, but the damage is already done: The bad news is in the living room going around on the hi-fi set at 33⅓ rpm.

The elements that would come to characterize all counter-

cultural events were popularized by the Beatles: unisex, the cele-
bration of dope, Surrealism built out of the scraps of everyday
life ("I Am the Walrus"), the Dada insult ("We're more popular
than Jesus Christ"), self-parody, and a steadfast refusal to take anything seriously (for "serious" read straight-faced, earnest, and
humorless). When the Beatles released "Revolution 1" (a put-down
of Mao's Red Book–carrying revolutionaries), the underground
press, which had gone heavily politico in the last years of the
sixties, accused them of having SOLD OUT! But the Beatles have
always been faithful, in their fashion, to the kids who buy their
records; they closed the decade with an image more universally
popular among the young than that of the Red Guard: the Hairy
Freak. In "Come Together" they presented us with the archetypal
hairy hippy of the most frozen-minded editorial writer's bad-trip
nightmares. It's a put-on, sure, done with self-parody and wit, but
underneath there's the serious invitation to the kids to get together
around the freak—the image the Beatles have used to personify
the emerging "counter" culture.

Bob Dylan's work might be divided, roughly, into three periods.
The first is of ballads and blues in the folk idiom, and clear, issue-
bound protest songs about such easily identifiable evils as war and
racism (he wrote all, with one or two exceptions, the good straight
protest songs of the sixties). The second period could be labeled,
without stretching the word a bit, "Surrealist." The mass-media
commentators, hard-pressed to say something that would sound
intelligent about the songs of this period, often used the word
"personal." But Dylan's imagery is not personal in the sense that
Yeats's or Blake's imagery is personal; there is no self-contained
symbol system which, once understood, will illumine "hidden"
meanings. He works, rather, with the Surrealist technique of
"radical juxtaposition":[12] laying side by side weirdly different
elements, usually images of American everyday life juxtaposed
with images of horrifying bizarreness. We find, for example, Jack
the Ripper at the head of the Chamber of Commerce, a business-
man looking for a market for a third world war. The tension between the ordinary element and the weird element strikes deeper
than the conscious level of the mind and ripples out in many direc-

tions like a pebble dropped into water: the effect attempted by all Surrealist art, an effect which Dylan has thoroughly mastered.

Dylan's third period might be called, with some caution, "allegorical." The music and lyrics are pared down and simplified, the American setting replaced by a timeless land peopled by an archetypal crew of hobos, drifters, thieves, con men, and gamblers who act out strange allegories which seem like hip passion plays. But the allegory is not simple and does not lend itself to one-to-one interpretation. The method remains that of Surrealism, but now the "ordinary, everyday" element is not stated but is supplied in the mind of the listener, who must attempt to make the connection between the bizarre happenings in the songs and his own personal situation. It is obvious that, given Dylan's Surrealistic method, there are as many interpretations for his songs as there are listeners. But it seems indicative of the mood of young people in the sixties that Dylan should achieve immense popularity with songs full of images of obscene horrors, despair, nihilism, entrapment, revolt, death, and apocalypse.

Dylan is the direct inheritor of the Beat tradition of total protest. His album *Highway 61 Revisited* is the most devastating and beautiful poetic indictment of the social order since Ginsberg's "Howl." What Kerouac had done for the hip disaffiliates of the fifties, chronicling their life style in *On the Road* and *The Subterraneans,* Dylan did for the hip disaffiliates who spanned the transitional years between the Beats and the "love generation." This was an uneasy period, marked by the involvement of white youth in the civil rights movement, the extension of drugs out of the ghetto and into the college campuses (and into the "underground" communities of non-students which were growing up around college campuses), the public awareness of the "dropout" phenomenon. In the early years of that period Dylan got to know life in the streets by the first-hand experience of trying to make it in New York City. For many of us Dylan's *Blonde on Blonde* embodies the whole "feel" of those restless years of dropping out, wandering, being lost and alone, trying drugs, living in a top-floor cold-water apartment on the edge of some college campus, making and unmaking uneasy sexual alliances: searching.[13]

And now Dylan's images are as indispensable to America's young as were the images of classical mythology to educated Englishmen of a hundred years ago: Look at the underground press, college papers, the political and critical statements of the young, and there seems to be a Dylan quote for every occasion, every mood, every current idea. Dylan has always seemed to have the uncanny ability to articulate thoughts that were in everybody's mind, always seemed to be one step ahead of where *you* happened to be. His career has been stormy; all the way back to his "electric" Newport appearance there have been those who accused him of the ultimate crime: having SOLD OUT! Throughout, Dylan remained remote and enigmatic, his interviews (the one in *Rolling Stone* is no exception) elaborate Dada put-ons, his "message" confined to his songs and the occasional poetic liner-notes to his records. He continued to grow in stature, to emerge (despite Albert Grossman, despite Columbia Records, despite the Dylan cults) as the most powerful artist of the contemporary American youth culture.

DOPE

"Surrealism" is a word I have used frequently in discussing the music of the Beatles and Bob Dylan; it also describes most of the rock of the sixties. It is one thing for this phenomenon to appear among a small group of European intellectuals living in tense, often disastrous, social conditions, but it is another thing for it to emerge as a guiding force in the popular music of affluent America's young people. It is obvious that any direct link to the Surrealist movement is tenuous, to say the least (most rock musicians are lucky if they've heard of Kerouac, let alone André Breton). One of the keys to explaining the presence of this strong Surrealist element in rock is the psychedelic drug experience.

There is a functional similarity between psychedelic drug experience and the "mind-bending" (to use a favorite mass-media word) art of the Surrealists. As Patrick Waldberg notes: "Through all those vociferations, refusals and deliberate absurdities, they [the Surrealists] were seeking a guiding light, a way to make a new truth dawn. A distrust of rationalism and formal convention . . . prompted the young men towards the exploration of the realm of the unconscious and the dream. They were seeking what might be called 'the language of the soul,' that is, the expression—stripped of all logical device—of the profound 'me' in its nakedness." [14] The young people of the sixties had picked up the Beat "distrust of rationalism and formal convention"; guilty and restless because of their "training" in the disintegrating bourgeois family, they sought "a way to make a new truth dawn." Mildly in marijuana, strongly in LSD, they found a way to explore "the realm of the unconscious and the dream" in search of "the profound 'me' in its nakedness." What the Surrealist had attempted, America's children found in drugs, which (in the proper set and setting) impose a "radical juxtaposition" on perception. It is not in the least surprising that the art of the Surrealists and the art of the youth of the sixties should be remarkably similar. [15]

THE GREAT HAIR STRUGGLE AND UNISEX

1964 was the year of "Beatlemania"; it was also the year that the "hair problem," as a British phenomenon, reached public consciousness in the States. By September, 1964, the subject merited an article in the Sunday magazine of *The New York Times*. Anthony Carthew, commenting on what was still seen as a uniquely British problem, wrote: "If . . . you are on the outside of this movement, you will find difficulty in distinguishing between the sexes. From the back, hair, pants and shoes seem identical. The carefully fostered public parade of the differences between boy and girl is apparently over. The two sides have reached a compromise." [16] Carthew's treatment was flippant, his explanation for the long-hair phenomenon simplistic: The kids were emulating rock stars (Beatles, *et al.*) who grew their hair long (1) because of a reaction to their service experience, and/or (2) because they had been, for the most part, students before they got into the rock business, and students have traditionally had long hair.

In December, 1964, the *Times* carried a report of what (to my knowledge) was the first widely publicized American hair case, that of Edward T. Kores, a fifteen-year-old suspended from Westbrook (Connecticut) High School for his (by 1970 standards extremely conservative) bangs. [17] Within two years "hair" cases were becoming numerous and the mass media had coined the word "unisex." *Newsweek* recognized the existence of this phenomenon with a full-page story, which included the now-classic mass-media formulation of the reason for unisex clothing in a quote from a Dr. Bruce Buchenholz: "It alleviates their anxiety. They can say he/she is not that different from me and thus it becomes easier for them to establish a relationship."[18] In 1968, *Life* gave us a major unisex article. The standard flippant treatment is still present, but a new element has crept in, a grudging acceptance, because it has finally dawned on somebody somewhere that there is money to be made.[19]

In October, 1968, the Supreme Court refused to hear a hair case (a suit brought by the parents of three boys expelled from a Dallas high school for wearing Beatle haircuts). Justice Douglas, as *The New York Times* predictably put it, issued a "sharp dissent": "It comes as a surprise that in a country where the states are restrained by an equal protection clause, a person can be denied education in a public school because of the length of his hair. I suppose that a nation bent on turning out robots might insist that every male have a crew cut and every female wear pigtails. . . ."[20] By the end of the sixties the courts were jammed with a backlog of hair cases, and even in the remotest towns of the Midwest, American boys were markedly hairier than ten years before; in the radical enclaves of Boston, New York, and San Francisco males with shoulder-length hair were common enough that only tourists from Kansas bothered to stop and stare.

To close the sixties we have the spectacle of Rudi Gernreich putting out a fashion line without sex differentiation[21] and the clothing manufacturers caught in capitalism's classical bind of having to sell what is antithetical to its values: Isadore Barmash, in the financial section of *The New York Times*, wrote: "Because there are some intriguing questions of changing sexual mores raised by the trend [unisex], more than a few retailers who are cashing in on it are embarrassed by it. They do not want to appear to encourage a cross-over of the sexes. . . .They do, however, want to tap what is developing as an important new market."[22] Paul Ressler, identified as "a manufacturer who has been in the forefront of the unisex movement in apparel," comes off with maybe the only intelligent comment on the subject to appear in the mass media to date: "Personally, I think that the unisex trend has nothing to do with manufacturers. It represents a demand from the sidewalks."[23]

CONCLUSION

Somehow, in the sixties, things became possible again. It became possible, first of all, to reject, as an isolated individual act, all the expectations and plans of the fifties. After weeks of sleepless nights and inner misery, I dropped out of college. Within a year I was meeting friends who had also dropped out. We made grim jokes about the situation we were in, which seemed to us then . . . nowhere. In 1964, the year of the Beatles, a bunch of crazy damn-fool kids my age went to Mississippi. I was sitting around, unemployed, in a youth ghetto in a college town, filling my time by reading Jung and writing a novel when I heard that three of those crazy kids had been killed in Mississippi; something turned over in my head: *They* had killed three of *us*. Then something else began to become possible—a sense of community. We were not isolated mad misfit children who refused to grow up; there were thousands of us, and we began to recognize each other. By 1968 I, an apolitical neo-Beatnik Orient freak, was working with an organization called the Resistance and playing a game called "paranoia" (Is your phone tapped? Do you think so-and-so is a fed?). By the end of the decade a huge number of America's young could no longer doubt their estrangement: WE ARE A SEPARATE PEOPLE. And this belief has also emerged aboveground: In his unquestionably adult and scholarly voice, Theodore Roszak argues in *The Making of a Counter Culture* that during the sixties youth culture turned into a "counter" culture diverging sharply from mainstream America.

The Dadaists, over fifty years ago, were staging "happenings" and guerrilla theater, reading poetry to music, and attacking bourgeois culture with everything from put-on to scurrilous insult. Although the Dadaists were artists they were, paradoxically, anti-art; Marcel Duchamp exhibited as "art," among other things, a bottle rack, a coal shovel, and a urinal. The Dadaist Hans Richter comments: "Of course, the bottle-rack and the urinal are not art. But the laughter that underlies this shameless exposure of 'all that is holy' goes so deep that a kind of topsy-turvy admiration sets in which applauds at its own funeral (the funeral, that is, of 'all that is holy'). We all share the feeling . . . that reality is nowhere to be found, not even in ourselves—that these bottle-racks and coal-shovels are only expressions of the emptiness of the world through which we stumble." [24]

These manufactured articles are, of course, perfect expressions of a commodity-dominated bourgeois society; Dada's attack upon "reality" is an attack on the reality of that society. Dada grew up in a time of vast revolutionary potential; there existed significant movements in opposition to class society, and Dada may be seen as an assault on its cultural values.

But with the death of revolutionary possibilities in Europe (sold out in Spain by a bourgeois-Communist coalition, crushed in Russia by the Bolshevik coup, etc.), Dada gave way to Surrealism, a movement already one step removed from change (the Dadaists were "doing" change, the Surrealists were thinking about it) with its searchings into the subconscious. As the bourgeois states consolidated themselves, Surrealism atrophied as a revolutionary movement. Individual Surrealists became orthodox Communists and thus were reabsorbed into the prevailing organization of appearances. Finally, Surrealism was completely transformed into bourgeois art as a commodity for sale (Salvador Dali, et al).

The reemergence of Dada and Surrealist elements (without, of course, those labels) in the youth culture of the sixties accompanied the reemergence of a growing opposition to bourgeois values (a pre-revolutionary movement). This opposition grew directly out of the contradictions built into American society: Push any of the institutions necessary to maintain American society far enough, and the negation of rather than the maintenance of that society is produced. Traditionally, the bourgeois family has been based upon sharply divided sex roles, but the social order that needs the bourgeois family to produce the kind of people who will maintain it also creates forces that cause the blending of sex roles.

As Jules Henry points out: "Most people do the job they have to do regardless of what they want to do; technological drivenness has inexorable requirements, and the average man or woman either meets them or does not work."[25] The jobs available are part of a vast, impersonal machine which produces useless commodities. Thus, "Deprived in his work life of personality aspirations, the American father reaches deeply into the emotional resources of his family for gratification formerly considered womanly—the tenderness and closeness of his children."[26] But the old masculine values of the culture are still strong in his mind, introjected from his own childhood when the bourgeois family was on firmer ground: "Since fathers cannot abandon their efforts to control children (and even wives), because the consequences of yielding entirely seem too grave, the man is caught between his need for gratifying his tender impulses and the requirement that he be an old-fashioned authority figure, too."[27] The result is the universally beloved American image: Dagwood Bumstead, the bumbling, ineffectual male who periodically is driven to create a show of masculine force which neither his wife nor his children take seriously.

But as the American father turns to his family for gratification, he finds his wife there ahead of him searching desperately for her own lost self: "Because nowadays both parents are concerned more and more with the gratification of their own impulses and with a variety of emotional yearnings, father and mother are thrown into collision."[28] In the deadly competition for the affection of their children the father's occasional playing of the traditional masculine game of authority and lawgiver, and his wife's occasional playing of the traditional feminine role of submissive domestic servant, are seen by the children as sham. It is not surprising, then, as Henry notes, that "many expressions of traditional masculinity and femininity are now felt by children to be intolerable."[29] And it is not surprising that boys and girls in the sixties began to dress and act more alike than ever before and that a vigorous feminist movement is growing up which aims at destroying the remnants of traditional sex roles. Thus the disintegration of the bourgeois family is producing children who are little inclined to reproduce the bourgeois family.

Similarly, as Henry has pointed out, American society needs

people with little control over their impulses for gratification in order to have enough customers for the useless products it needs to sell to maintain its economic system. But stress that drive toward impulse release efficiently enough, and you produce young people who will have little incentive to work at an ungratifying job. American society needs schizophrenic people with an infinite ability to split themselves (a "work" mind and a "play" mind, a mask for every occasion, etc.) in order to fit into a society that treats people as objects to be placed, at the will of the managers, wherever they are needed in the huge machine that is busy grinding out useless commodities. But teach this fragmentation efficiently enough, and you (besides increasing the number of clinically defined schizophrenics in mental institutions[30]) produce young people who are attracted to drugs—which relate the fragments and, through the "radical juxtaposition" of the Surrealists and Dadaists, make the connection between those fragments—and learn to see themselves as whole people on a whole earth. In short, when the society becomes absurd enough, people will begin rejecting it in toto. And that is precisely what has happened; there are now huge numbers of young people who are thoroughly alienated from every aspect of mainstream American life.

Walking the tightrope into the void created by the necessity of transforming *all* values (necessary if we wish even to *survive*) can become so painful that many young people jump off. The popular mass-media contention that those hell-raising students or dropped-out hippies will end up raising kids in the suburbs is true for some, perhaps even many. But others will spin off into the dead ends of old leftist positions which offer pseudo-answers and the illusion of opposition (Progressive Labor party, Trotskyite splinters, etc.), continue the gambit of looking to other cultures for meaning (the Weatherman, with its doctrine of "follow Third World leadership"), attempt in rural communes the impossible (and irrelevant) task of re-creating pioneer America complete with sharply defined sexual roles (it always seems easier, if present values have become meaningless, to try to rebuild a lost, "golden" past than it is to create new values), or make a fetish of the counter culture itself and talk of a "new nation" just at a point in history when it is becoming clear that what is not needed are "new" nations (the old ones may yet kill us all).

But, it seems to me, increasing numbers of young people will not be able to take any of those dead-end roads. I think the parallels between the American youth counter culture and the Dada movement are uncannily strong. A single thread runs through all their diverse and often confusing manifestations: Both movements share a thorough dedication to personal freedom and self-fulfillment and a total distrust of authorities of whatever variety. A comment of Hans Richter's on the Dadaists applies equally well to America's burgeoning counter culture and, as the contradictions of American society continue to emerge, will be even more apt for the seventies: "There was a revolution going on, and Dada was right in the thick of it. At one moment they were all for the *Spartakus* movement; then it was Communism, Bolshevism, Anarchism and whatever else was going. But there was always a side-door left open for a quick getaway, if this should be necessary to preserve what Dada valued most—personal freedom and independence."[31]

Chapter 3

UNIVERSITY REFORM

The Meaning of the Campus Struggle

Most Americans are confused about the protests and disorders that have become regular features of the academic year. The dramas played out at San Francisco State, Columbia, Stanford, MIT, Michigan State, Kent State, Jackson State, Wisconsin, and Harvard have become the subject of interminable research, books, television programs, and government investigations. This plethora of analysis has been responsible for much of the confusion in the public mind concerning campus unrest. Depending on the purpose of the author, analyses have blamed disorders on the war in Vietnam, permissive upbringing, Communist conspiracies (or at least subversive radicals), weak-kneed administrators, and even the normal spring-time libidinal urges of young people. To say the least, few of these explanations have been convincing.

A study by the Urban Research Corporation of Chicago goes a long way toward shattering a number of myths.[1] First, it is not a small hard core of students who have been involved. In the first six months of 1969 (the period most studied by writers on the subject), URC found that at least 215,000 students participated in protests. Second, 76 percent of the protests resulted in no destruction or violence, 60 percent did not interrupt college routine, and non-negotiable demands were presented in only 6 percent of the incidents. The study further found that war-related protests were less numerous than those centering on racial issues or "student power" demands. The draft was a major factor in only 1 percent of all protests; but 49 percent of the protests centered on racial issues, 42 percent on student-power issues, and only 25 percent on antiwar or antimilitary issues. (The percentages total more than

100 because many protests were over more than one issue.) Far from being weak-kneed, college administrators refused to accept 69 percent of all demands and had 3,652 students arrested, 956 suspended, and 708 placed on probation. Finally, the New Left was found to have participated in only 28 percent of all protests.

This data, which contradicts the glib impressions of most of those charged with informing the public, goes a long way in revealing the true nature of student unrest. However, there are a few more stumbling blocks to understanding. Most of the causal theories espoused by various commentators are demonstrably wrong. We will deal with these theories before going on to consider the true causes of disruptions and other aspects of the student movement.

FALSE STARTS

In the first category of "wrong" analyses we find the Freudian and hard-core minority theories. The Freudian analysis sees student discontent as being a manifestation of the Oedipus complex: College administrators assume the role of father in the university setting, leading the students to hate the administrators as they would their fathers. Despite the attractiveness of the theory for a psychoanalysis-conscious nation, it fails to be of much use because it does not explain why, since the Oedipal relationship has supposedly existed all along, we have witnessed a sudden upsurge of student disorders.

The hard-core minority theory has gained more currency than the Freudian approaches among the public and government officials. The theory holds that student disorders are the work of a small, well-organized group of dissidents, either controlled by subversives or carrying out their own subversive plans. The rest of the college population is typified as being unsympathetic to the aims of the rebels. But for this hard core of troublemakers, the campuses would presumably be peaceful.

The advocates of this theory are correct when they say that most students are not revolutionaries. In a survey for CBS News, Daniel Yankelovich, Inc., found that only 1 percent of the student population could be categorized as radical dissidents. However, the percentage of students participating in demonstrations has increased from 7 percent in the school year 1966–67 to 28 percent in 1968–69, according to the Gallup pollsters.[2] This may still be a minority, but it is far more significant than the hard-core theorists presume.

The hard-core minority theory has other failings. It is the common characteristic of conspiracy theories to attribute to the "conspirators" unusual powers over the masses or the defenseless young. By some means this hard core is able to dupe unsuspecting people into supporting their causes; once involved, the innocent are merely used and then discarded. But if a tiny group of people could instigate disruptions in schools across the country involving significant numbers of students, they would surely be the greatest political organizers in history. Certainly a small group can be effective in advocating a position, but it is only as influential as its ideas are powerful. The supplemental Kerner Commission reports refuted the hard-core minority theory with regard to civil disorders, and even the FBI agrees that the theory does not explain student disruptions.[3]

In another category are the theories of gross exaggeration propounded by professors and radical students. Many professors view college disruptions as a neo-McCarthyism, a fascism of the left. They see the assault on their privileges and prerogatives as anti-intellectual in nature and a threat to academic freedom. For these professors, the only solution is to isolate disrupters from the campus.

Certainly a number of student disruptions have taken on anti-democratic features, and a number of groups are quite willing to sacrifice academic freedom to the attainment of their political goals, but to characterize the basically amorphous student movement in these terms is absurd. While student opposition to a riot-control course at Harvard or a lecture on the genetic inferiority of Negroes at Dartmouth may have been threatening, it seems strange that professors fear being asked to justify their choices. Without such justifications, how can courses be judged to be within or outside of the humanitarian principles of the academy?

On the student side, current disruptions and massive antiwar protests are seen as the swelling manpower of a revolutionary youth movement. In this exaggerated view, the thousands of protesting students are the militant vanguard of an imminent revolution that lacks only the spark to set it off.

Youth unrest may be widespread, but it certainly has yet to reach revolutionary proportions; nor have many of the young acquired revolutionary consciousness. The same Yankelovich survey that found widespread student unrest also found a basic underlying commitment to work for change within the present system. Some 43 percent of the young strongly agree and another 46 percent partially agree that the American system of representative democracy can respond effectively to the needs of the people. Despite the incantations of professors and student revolutionaries, the student movement has so far refrained from becoming either demagogic or revolutionary in nature.

THE ROOTS OF UNREST

If none of the previous descriptions explains student unrest, what does? A first step on the path to answering that question might be to point out that student disorders are not a new phenomenon—there have always been disorders on college campuses. The relationships within the university and between the university and society have been evolving for hundreds of years, and students in the past were often rowdy and demanding.[4] The important issue is not why campus disruptions occur in general but why student disorders are suddenly sweeping the nation.

At the root of these disorders is a crisis of authority. The crisis has two main elements: the feeling among young people that the political system is not pursuing the proper goals and their feeling of alienation and futility because they have no voice in determining policy. It is this helplessness that causes young people, particularly students, to engage in their various forms of deviating behavior. In making demands for dramatic changes in policy or for a redistribution of power within the system, students are not merely attempting to discredit those in authority. They are attempting to define the terms under which they will renew their consent for the system to continue to rule.

Bruno Bettelheim, in *Obsolete Youth,* suggests one possible cause of the crisis of authority. He argues that society now, unlike in the past, keeps the next generation too long in a state of dependency, and many young people rebel against this artificially prolonged childhood: "What they want is to find their manhood." [5] Furthermore, as psychologist Erik Erikson told a gathering of scholars invited to the White House to discuss student unrest, there is "an ethical yearning" among the young today: They see a brilliantly capable society using its brilliance to perfect its capacity for overkill without the slightest qualms. This restlessness, which is apparent in student leaders, becomes even more manifest in moments of crisis, when it is possible to motivate the majority of normally passive young people.

The frustrations caused by this prolonged dependency should be explanation enough for all those parents who, having worked hard so that their children would have it better than they did, question why young people insist on going out into the ugly world by themselves. It is not to rebel against their parents, but rather to become themselves: independent, thinking, important people. To the extent that any person in authority acts in such a way as to prolong this dependency or make the young person's powerlessness any more painful, he sets himself up for rebellion.

Young people have not always been subjected to this extended dependency. At the turn of the century children reached physical maturity at age sixteen or seventeen, went to work, got married and raised a family. Today physical maturity, as gauged by the age of pubescence in girls, has dropped to 12.6 years of age. At the same time, compulsory schooling, college, military service, minimum age requirements for obtaining employment, and a host of other practices have pushed the marriage age beyond eighteen years and in many cases to twenty-one or twenty-two, the age at which students graduate from college. Even more important, though, is that for six or more years young people are physically able to assume the same responsibilities their grandparents assumed, yet do not do so for a variety of societal reasons.

Held in the unwanted dependency and denied any real power over their lives by voting-age requirements and overprotective parents, young people rebel. They strike first at what they consider to be the worst evils of the system, and then at the legitimacy of the system that makes such decisions and also excludes young people from its processes. It is this two-pronged attack that we will now consider: the specific issues raised by students, and their demand for the right to participate in the decisions that affect their lives.

INSTITUTIONS IN NEED OF REFORM

One could hardly pick a more likely place than the university for the crisis of authority to first become apparent. The universities contain a critical mass of unwilling dependents and an institutional structure infamous for its anachronisms. As John Gardner has said, the university is able to criticize others but is unable to renew itself. The most important question has become: What is the purpose of the university?

The public attitude toward the purpose of a college education still reflects the thinking of a generation preoccupied with guaranteeing financial security. If in the first third of the century college was viewed as a nursery for rich adolescents, in the second third it was seen as a supermarket for jobs and marriages. A survey of adult opinion by Angus Campbell and William C. Eckerman, of the University of Michigan's Survey Research Center, found that 71 percent of respondents thought college was more important now because of tougher job competition and demands for higher skills. Only 7 percent cited the need of the individual for a liberal understanding of the world and its peoples.

This view of college as a career factory is reinforced on all sides by the schools, the government, the parents. The potential high school dropout is warned to get his diploma because his lifetime earning power will then be $275,000 rather than $150,000. If he goes on to college he is assured that his earnings will be $470,000. College then is seen as a good financial investment. A capital expenditure of $10,000 will return almost fifty-fold over a lifetime. That beats the stock market!

Far from sharing this viewpoint, many students today would lament with William Graham Sumner, the nineteenth-century economist, that "the great American dream is universal education. [But] the great American tragedy is that education is confused with schooling." In their rededication to the academy as a place for scholarship and the broadening of understanding, students might agree with Alfred North Whitehead that "the justification for a university is that it preserves the connection between knowledge and zest of life, by uniting the young and the old in the imaginative consideration of learning. The university imparts information, but it imparts it imaginatively. At least this is the function which it should perform for society. A university which fails in this respect has no reason for existence." [6]

If we accept Whitehead's definition, we must conclude that most universities do fail: because of their job-training-school attitude, because they have become prisons for many students. Kingman Brewster, president of Yale, has pointed out that there are many unwilling students in universities. They are there because of the threat of the draft or because their parents feel they must have a degree to "make it" in the world. They persevere in a community that teeters under their burden and fails to interest them. Further, with nearly 50 percent of young people going on to college, there is a real question of whether a college education, as presently conceived, is meaningful for those in the lower half of the intelligence scale. The constant exhortations to young people that everyone should go to college seem ludicrous when many of those presently attending would much prefer a different type of experience.

Nor is the cause of restoring the academy well served by the changing role of professors. At a time when their value to students is highest, professors are increasingly fleeing from their teaching duties. Whether frightened off by the "publish or perish" threat or lured away by the consulting gambit, academics are defecting from the classroom and into research or lucrative jobs with government, business, or foundations.

As a result students suffer from professional neglect or, at best, the teaching of graduate students. This situation is compounded by the fact that even as more young people go into college teaching, the increase in the number of students is greatly outpacing them. About 15,000 Ph.D.'s are produced each year, which is fewer than half the number needed to maintain a 1-to-10 ratio of teachers to students. In part this is because the teaching profession remains a closed shop. Without a doctorate a professor is continually discriminated against, so the degree is pursued with a mixture of vigor and cynicism. In the end the Ph.D. is seen as a license restricted to those who survive a process designed to limit the number of survivors.

The problem of teacher shortages can be solved in part by bringing more non-academics from the world of affairs into the university to replace consultant-professors. However, in the long run the answer lies in redefining the qualifications that a professor must meet. Certainly the insistence on having a Ph.D., and the survival course required to obtain one, can be dramatically changed to correspond with reality.

Another important issue is the organization of the curriculum. There is a growing movement among students against the concept of a restricted major or field of concentration. Instead of these unimaginative groupings of courses and emphases, students seek to create their own plan of study. There has been little success at this effort, although required survey courses are giving way under the pressure. This effort is actually restorative; the specialization of course work is a product of the late nineteenth century, and education before that was much more personally tailored.

Perhaps of more concern to those outside the university is the movement toward abolishing grades. This seems a wildly irresponsible idea to those who view college as a job-training experience. A great number of teachers, however, favor the move because real academic study is undermined if a student cares only what his grade on his final exams will be. With grades rather than education as the objective, many students are encouraged to play along with the system—taking easy courses or cramming at the last minute to remember facts that will be as quickly forgotten. Such tactics, though understandable given the educational context, work to destroy any sense of intellectual curiosity and to confine the student to areas of study in which he is already adept. It is ironic that the rationale for grades is that good marks in college ensure a superior professional career later on. A paper by Dr. Philip Price published in the *Journal of Medical Education* in 1964 directly challenges this contention. Price's study concludes that performance in school, as measured by grade-point averages, is almost completely unrelated to all the factors having to do with performance as a physician. The same results, one would suspect, hold for lawyers, teachers, and everyone else.

These are just some of the basic issues with which universities have failed to deal and which represent the underpinning of the student protest movement—efforts intended to return academics to academia. There are other traditional issues that go more to the heart of authority in the university. The student's most obvious grievance is symbolized in the words *in loco parentis*. Through the use of this legal vagary, universities have taken upon themselves the responsibility to regulate a great part of a student's non-academic life. Curfews, visiting hours, bans on alcohol and drugs have all been instituted for the purpose of protecting students from a number of life's experiences. Some of the restrictions are ludicrous vestiges of the Victorian age, such as curfews for women but not men, dormitories located in such a way as to provide as much open space as possible between women and men, and requirements that doors be left open at least the width of a book. Such rules are about as effective as they were in Victoria's day.

Schools have been recalcitrant in changing these rules, and so more and more students have been seeking living quarters off-campus. Such rules, argues National Student Association president Ed Schwartz, "are resented not because they are unreasonable—which they are—but because they are disrespectful." One student made an even stronger case to a *Life* reporter: "I've fought for civil rights in Mississippi, and I've spent the past three summers setting my own rules. I'm responsible for the college magazine and I control a $5,000 budget. Why should a dean decide whether I can drink in my dormitory room or when I have to take my dates home?" This question not only raises the issue of arbitrary rules, but also the right of a college to make them.

Colleges will argue that they have a responsibility to the student's parents to enact the rules, or that they are required to do so by state laws. Both answers are inadequate. Authority relationships between parents and children do not require the intervention of a university. The surrogate parental role is more often assumed by the universities, not forced upon them by parents.

There is no reason why universities should be invested with powers to control the social lives of students. Whatever regulations are necessary can be determined by those most concerned—the students. The case for student power is most obvious in the issue of social regulations. Here the adoption of enlightened policies is not enough; the university must surrender these powers to the students.

The question of student rights has provoked a number of controversies over rights that the average person takes for granted. It was only a few years ago that a federal court in Missouri ruled that students have a right to due process in disciplinary procedures that might lead to their expulsion.[7] It was only in February, 1969, that the Supreme Court held, in *Tinker v. School Board of Des Moines,* that students possess all the rights of the First Amendment within certain limitations. The issue in the Tinker case centered on the right of high-school students to wear black armbands in protest of the war in Vietnam. However, it might also have concerned the freedom of students to publish underground newspapers, for the student press to go uncensored, or for students to dress or wear their hair as they please.

New York City was one of the first school systems to respond positively to this ruling. The city's Board of Education has produced a bill of rights for high-school students which, although branded as unacceptable by some civil-libertarian and activist groups, is significant. The proposals would provide student control over student activity funds, student participation in curriculum and discipline decisions, and student publications generally free of censorship; would protect political rights; would eliminate all restrictions governing dress and appearance except those concerning safety; and would institute a system of hearings and due process in disciplinary actions. This is a big step for high schools, which have been notoriously repressive. It would also represent a significant change if adopted by the universities.

The most crucial issue involving student participation concerns the extent of student involvement in decisions relating to curriculum, hiring of faculty, and the selection of university administrators. On the first two questions, students and faculty often clash head-on. Faculty members see their prerogatives to decide course content and to control with administrators the hiring of faculty to be the essence of academic freedom. Student attempts to become involved in either process are viewed as attacks upon this freedom and therefore threats to the life of the university. In both instances faculty members are guilty of taking an extreme position in order to discredit the opposition. Certainly there are students, and faculty too, who would like to mold the curriculum to fit their own political outlook and to appoint faculty who share that outlook. However, neither of these groups represents the dominant opinion on the issue.

The demand for student involvement stems from the view that students have a vital interest in decisions on what will be taught and who will be appointed to the faculty. Too often student opinion is neglected in deciding whether a certain course or field of study will be added or dropped. The decision is usually a matter of economy or convenience for the faculty or administration. Also, students have a direct interest in whether "needed" faculty will be appointed and whether faculty members will devote their time to teaching or to research. Some professors retort that student involvement might destroy the "publish or perish" dictum but would replace it with an equally tyrannical "be popular or perish" requirement. Taken in the extreme, such might well be the case, but if considered in the form suggested by students it is an unlikely occurrence.

A number of schools have already taken steps toward student involvement. Many faculty and administrative committees call upon students for consultations. However, that is not enough. The argument that "any good student idea will be heard" is simply false. What it really means is that any student idea the faculty or administration likes will be heard. Meaningful student participation requires a vote as well as a voice. Students who are to be serious partners in decision making must have equal powers, must be present during all deliberations, and must participate in votes. This is not a call for student-run universities, for it is generally agreed that on matters of curriculum and hiring the student voice should be a minority voice, but it is a call for the recognition of students as equally important participants in operating the university.

Another major argument against student participation is that it would result in the politicizing of the educational process. This charge is specious. Every faculty or administrative committee is already permeated with politics. Members are chosen because they represent certain shades of opinion, and not for their objectivity. Also, it is well known that such committees do not take formal votes but rely on consensus. The addition of students might make consensus more difficult, and well it should, but it certainly would not politicize decision making any more than it already is.

The question of selecting administrators is much more difficult. The majority of decisions in the university are not made by committees but by a host of administrators from the president down to department heads. The problem is how to make these decisions the desires of the total academic community. Since the prerogative of selecting administrators usually rests with alumni-dominated boards of trustees or state governing boards, the university tends to be very responsive to the interests of these boards, sometimes to the detriment of members of the institution. For this reason, it is argued, students and faculty should pick administrators.

Kingman Brewster has attempted a different resolution of this problem. Instead of subjecting university presidents to constant popularity checks, he suggests that they be appointed to specified terms of office which can be extended if their work is judged satisfactory; in this way they can be held accountable for their work. This certainly would be an improvement over the current policy of appointing presidents for indefinite terms, but it is not enough; it would merely mean that the boards of trustees would review their own appointees. Both students and faculty as well as the public and alumni representatives should share in the responsibility of selecting such important officials as the president of a university. Then when the time came for evaluating the performance of the man, each group would be asked to present its judgment. Until such a system is adopted, methods should be developed through which criticism and sanctions can be directed toward an administrator who does not satisfactorily perform his job.

An experiment at the University of Puget Sound might well bear copy by other schools. After the threat of a student strike, the trustees agreed to a student-government demand that students choose the dean of students. In the end the method chosen by the students did provide for the involvement of faculty and administrators, but the students could nominate a man sympathetic to their problems. College administrations must be made more accountable, and deans of students across the nation should be chosen by means devised by the students themselves.

These are not the only issues of contention on campus, although they are probably the most fundamental. The crisis of authority has manifested itself in many forms, but the one that has commanded the attention of the news media are the demands by extremist factions that seek not to restore the academy, but rather to change it radically. It is to these factions that we now turn our attention.

Two Radical Groups

Of all the contesting groups on campus, white radicals and black students have made the biggest impression on the public consciousness. As the Urban Research Corporation found, disruptions, which make headlines, were more likely in protests in which New Left groups participated, and black student organizations were involved in 51 percent of all protests. It is not possible here to consider *all* the peculiarities of these two factions of the student movement, but some description may be useful to understanding.

Although there are independent socialist groups, the main thrust of white radical politics on campus has been led by the Students for a Democratic Society (SDS). While all SDS members share a belief in revolution as the only way to end economic exploitation, racism, and American imperialism, factions differ as to method. Since the major split in the organization in 1969, the most important factions are the Worker-Student Alliance, backed by the doctrinaire Progressive Labor party, which advocates alliance with the working class in strikes and by community organizing; and the New Left caucus, notably the Weatherman (named for the lyrics of a Bob Dylan song). The Weatherman holds that revolution must be based on an alliance of students and blacks and is willing to use violence as a means of inspiring revolutionary consciousness among the masses.

To the demands by such groups, which are aimed at breaking the link between the university and the State and Defense Departments, college administrators are likely to respond that the institution is politically neutral. What they fail to realize is that deciding not to continue doing something is no more political than deciding to do it in the first place.

The dangerous aspect of radicalism on campus is its doctrine of violence. The Cox Commission on the Columbia disorders of 1968 argued that violence is unacceptable because it endangers reason and civility, it may lead to escalation of force, and it threatens the survival of the free university itself; the commission concluded that the whole university community must unite to condemn the use of force by anybody. Surely the experience of Berkeley is testament enough that meeting violence with even more massive official violence neither resolves crises nor prevents future conflict.

Black students, only recently found in large numbers on college campuses, have become strident advocates of change. These changes are often reformist, seeking the correction of centuries-old racism in admissions, curricula, faculty hiring, and general employment. Black student activism is a fairly revolutionary change. In the past, black students, mostly middle-class, entered white schools to participate in white society on its terms. With the emergence of the black power and Black Is Beautiful movements, this assimilating process is gradually being rejected. More and more working-class blacks are going to college, and they reject the "Uncle Toms" and "Sambos" of the past. The emphasis is on black solidarity and identity, and the black student might reject whites altogether. There are now black student organizations and cultural centers on the order of the Hillel Houses for Jewish students and Newman Centers for Catholics.

The call for black studies programs (dealing with the African and Afro-American experiences) has often been met by arguments questioning the necessity or usefulness of such programs. In the April, 1969, issue of the *Atlantic Monthly,* Professor DeVere E. Pentony, a dean at San Francisco State, cogently defended the new program: "The argument is that if there is to be an exodus from the land of physical and psychological bondage, an informed and dedicated leadership is needed to help bring about individual and group pride and a sense of cohesive community." This pride, Pentony continues, is to be achieved by studying the attainments of black individuals and civilizations of the past.

Another issue is whether or not black studies are to be taught exclusively by black professors and attended exclusively by black students. White professors, many blacks insist, are incapable of truly understanding the black experience, and white students are seen as "psychologically limiting" factors in the classroom, inhibiting discussion among blacks. But Roy Wilkins points out that separate-but-equal facilities are likely to be contested in the courts,[8] and Pentony argues that the value of such courses is to "tell it as it really is," and therefore they have value for students of all races.[9] Fortunately, this view has prevailed.

A further concern among black students is the university's relations with blacks outside the campus. Blacks are demanding more lenient admissions criteria so as to admit more black students, a halt to the schools' physical encroachment on black communities, and employment of black workers by the university and by its building contractors. Demands for hiring specific numbers of black workers have arisen on many campuses. One way to sidestep the sticky "quota" issue in hiring is to use the "goals" approach similar to the U.S. Labor Department's Philadelphia Plan.

Black participation in the campus struggle raises again the question of administrative responsiveness to the need for change. Black demands have tended to be reformist, but they have rarely been effective without black-led protests. Receptivity to black demands will prove to be a test of how amenable a university is to change of any kind.

BEYOND THE HORIZON

Certainly these few pages are scarcely enough to explain or judge the campus situation definitively. But one thing rings clear: The course of universities in the 1970s will be determined primarily by the members of the institutions themselves. Glib assertions that outsiders—transient radicals or government agents—exercise overwhelming control over academic communities are simply not convincing. A reexamination of the governing of universities with a keen eye to their capacity for change and accommodation will be necessary to restore the disorderly creativity that typifies the modern campus.

And what lies ahead? There will certainly be new issues, new demands, and new strains within the university. Environmental issues will claim a place in the curriculum, and women will provide the next social equality issue. But regardless of the specific issues, the challenge will be the same—the challenge of constant renewal—which is what the campus struggle is all about.

Chapter 4

YOUNG WORKERS

The Unconsidered Americans

With so much media attention focused on college students, the more numerous young workers have gone unnoticed, ignored by the opinion makers, ignored even by their own unions in many cases. They produce soldiers for Vietnam and taxes for the public treasury and it is assumed they are stable and content. But they are not. However inarticulate, they are resentful. Continuing to overlook their grievances could be dangerous for the society. In 1970 there were nearly 20 million people in the labor force under age twenty-five. Each year some 3 million persons enter the labor force, and of these, 1 million go to work as hourly-wage industrial workers, trade-union apprentices, and low-level management personnel. But they cannot really be said to enter a labor "movement," at least not in the old sense. All the sympathy that was once bestowed upon labor by the liberal and intellectual communities is now directed toward the New Left and the blacks. Inside the unions, a gerontocracy rules and the young struggle against the admonitions that they are too inexperienced to take part in the decision-making process.

Economic Insecurity

The truth is that many young workers are suffering discrimination within their unions and within society that is at least as severe as the expressed grievances of students, if not blacks. It is assumed by the educated middle and upper classes that workers today are well-off, but this opinion errs in regard to the young in the labor force. According to the Bureau of Labor Statistics, in

1969 the average worker with three dependents took home only $78.49 in 1957–59 dollars, as compared to $78.88 in 1965. This inflationary discrepancy is even greater for the young wage earner. The older workers have the better jobs, greater breaks at overtime pay, less likelihood of being laid off, and longer vacations.

The younger worker is caught in a squeeze. He pays taxes, unlike the very poor, and has all the aspirations of the middle class, not the least of which is a better education for his children than he got. He does all right financially so long as he is single, but when he gets married and has children his standard of living drops.

According to the Bureau of Labor Statistics, the income needs for a family with two children are almost 3.5 times the needs of a single individual. Typical blue-collar wages, however, increase only by two times during the years from twenty to thirty, when the average worker marries and begins raising his family. The young worker's expenses, therefore, will increase at a rate 1.5 times faster than his earning capacity. Unlike the older worker, whose wife often holds down a job and helps establish a middle-class economic status, the young worker lacks the extra breadwinner at the very time he has the added expense of growing children.

He very likely also has a mortgage. According to a 1967 poll by the Committee on Political Education (COPE) of the AFL-CIO, 75 percent of all union members under the age of forty live in the suburbs, and most are paying off mortgages with interest rates at over 8 percent. Brendan Sexton, a United Auto Workers analyst, states: "The young married worker 25 or 30 years old will probably make regular monthly payments half again as high as those paid by a worker of 40 or 45 years."[1] Small wonder that the young worker spends more than he earns and goes into debt on the average of more than $100 per year.

The tax structure, moreover, is not geared to help the young worker and his new family. Although married persons are given a more advantageous tax rate than single persons, this single-married distinction is not equal at all levels of income. For example, at a yearly income of $5,000, the difference between the tax rate for a married person and for a single person is only 2.0 percent. On an income of $7,000, the differential is 2.7 percent.

It is 3.7 percent for a $10,000 income. But for a yearly income of $20,000, an unlikely prospect for a blue-collar worker, the differential is 8.5 percent.

EMOTIONAL INSECURITY

If the young worker is in an economic bind, he also is in an emotional bind. He lacks the prestige of a college education, and, if white, the supportive spirit of any solidarity movement such as the black-power movement. He is not celebrated in song, motion picture, fiction. The columnist Pete Hamill observes: "Our novelists write about bullfighters, migrant workers, screenwriters, psychiatrists, failing novelists, homosexuals, advertising men, gangsters, actors, politicians, drifters, hippies, spies and millionaires; I have yet to see a work of the imagination deal with the life of a wirelather, a carpenter, a subway conductor, an ironworker or a derrick operator."[2]

In his shop or factory the young worker realizes that his labor is more tedious than that of many other Americans and that it probably will never be any more exciting or challenging than it is now. Moreover, in his daily routine he has little responsibility for his own work, an alienating factor that may bother him more than it bothered men in earlier eras when one felt lucky to have any work at all.

The age gap notable throughout society is especially pronounced in the unions. Because of the low birth rates during the Depression, followed some years later by the post–World War II baby boom, there will be about 1 million *fewer* persons in the 35–44 age bracket in 1975 than in 1965, but 8.75 million *more* in the 25–34 age bracket. This younger age group can expect a 62 percent growth rate in the 1965–80 period. The median age of the work force was 39.3 years in 1965; the projected median for 1980 is 35.9 years. The work force is coming to be composed of the young and the old.

In his own union the young worker has much less to say about policy than does his older co-worker. So far the young are relatively unrepresented in labor councils. George Meany, president of the AFL-CIO, celebrated his seventy-fifth birthday in 1970 and told reporters that he has no intention of retiring. A similar gap exists in most locals and is reflected in policy decisions. The prerogatives of seniority are preached with a sense of moral righteousness. If the union leadership chooses to press for higher pension payments rather than pay increases in contract negotiations, the young employee has to go along. If it chooses to press Congress for increased Social Security benefits, the cost of the payments, the young worker knows, will come out of his pocket.

One result of these frustrations among young workers has been greater militancy in seeking higher pay, a condition with which older labor leaders seem unable to deal. In 1969, 12 percent of all the contracts recommended by union negotiators met rejection in membership votes—down from 14 percent in 1968, but up from 8.7 percent in 1964, 10 percent in 1965, and 11.7 percent in 1966. The old-timers broke with the Johnson administration's proposed 3.2 percent guideline for wage increases, only to be told by their young membership that even 15 percent was not good enough.

As a former director of the Federal Mediation and Conciliation Service pointed out, "Many young workers who have grown up in a period of relative affluence have never experienced either a real depression or the early history of union struggles. Moreover, they are not very interested in attempts to acquaint them with these hard facts of earlier years. Many have never experienced a strike of any duration. When these facts are coupled with what may be loosely described as the current disillusionment of youth in other areas of activity, negative ratification votes are not surprising." But this official is missing the point of the contemporary reality: The young worker, relative to older workers and to his age mates elsewhere, is in an economic vise, and further, he lacks an adequate voice in his union to do anything about it.

POWERLESSNESS

The young worker—and we are speaking here of the white worker—also feels politically impotent. He sees privileged students who, he feels, have no respect for their country. They seem to be abetted by the courts, the rich, and the know-it-all intellectuals. Because they are the pets of society, the students, he feels, can get away with antisocial actions that would land him in jail if he tried them. And he notes the special help given blacks, such as relaxed college admittance standards and special job-training programs, and concludes that blacks really are privileged too, rather than deprived.

A *Newsweek* poll appearing in the October 6, 1969, issue described the reaction of America's white, blue-collar workers to black aspirations. This working-class cohort was defined as "families whose breadwinners have at most a high school education, hold blue-collar jobs, and bring home incomes of $5,000 to $10,000 a year. . . . They comprise 23 percent of the white population, nearly twice the black population, and a fifth of the total country." Seventy-nine percent of this group believed that blacks "could have done something" about living conditions in the slums—as compared with 63 percent of a white-collar sample. Nearly one-half—49 percent—of the blue-collar group said blacks actually have a better chance than they do to get a good job. Needless to say, blacks perceive the situation differently, but the whites' strength of feeling cannot be ignored.

Here, then, is the polarization of perceived grievances that led to the strong support given George Wallace by working people, particularly the young, in 1968. It is too simple to say that these people were racists—the angle employed by most of the media, whose reporters are usually drawn from the educated middle class. A more perceptive look came from Mike Hubbard, of the University of Michigan *Daily,* who talked with workers in the Wallace stronghold of Flint, Michigan. "Certainly these Americans do not identify with red-necked racism," Hubbard wrote. "No one ever taught them Negro history, but they grew up with blacks. . . . They don't dislike blacks, they just feel black men shouldn't be given a bigger break than anyone else. The white United Auto Workers members as a whole do not believe Wallace is a racist. All they know is what he told them, and he never said he hated blacks. Even the most militant Negro workers I talked to didn't feel there was large-scale prejudice in the union. They dislike Wallace, but not the men who are voting for him."[3]

In their study "Continuity and Change in American Politics:

Parties and Issues in the 1968 Election," Philip E. Converse and his associates point out the strong labor-union and youth support received by George Wallace. Outside the South, the percentage of white union members who preferred Wallace over Nixon or Humphrey was more than three times as great—19 percent versus 6 percent—as it was for non-union workers. In the South, 52 percent of those affiliated with the trade-union movement expressed a preference for Wallace, whereas only 28 percent of non-unionists supported him.

Wallace showed his greatest drawing power with the younger voter, capturing 13 percent of the vote among people under thirty outside the South, but only 3 percent of those over seventy. Wallace's strength thus increased directly with the degree of unionization and with the youth of the voter. As Converse *et al.* describe it:

> Although privileged young college students angry at Vietnam and shabby treatment of the Negro saw themselves as sallying forth to do battle against a corrupted and cynical older generation, a more head-on confrontation at the polls, if a less apparent one, was with their own age mates who had gone from high school off to the factory instead of college, and who were appalled by the collapse of patriotism and respect for the law that they saw about them. Outside of the election period, when verbal articulateness and leisure for political activism count most heavily, it was the college share of the younger generation—or at least its politicized vanguard—that was most prominent as a political force. At the polls, however, the game shifts to "one man, one vote," and this vanguard is swamped even within its own generation.[4]

Wallace's support among young workers was an expression of populism more than racism. He spoke to their frustrations with the educated, the liberals, with government and business, who seemed attuned to the plight of working-class blacks, but not of working-class whites. Robert Kennedy managed to show concern about both, and he had a great deal of support among both. After Kennedy's assassination, Wallace was the only politician left who seemed to care.

Tom Kahn, executive director of the League for Industrial Democracy, put it this way in the April, 1969, issue of the AFL-CIO publication, *The American Federationist:*

> Wallace articulated the belief of a considerable minority of less-than-securely-affluent working people that they were being made to bear the burden of financing a war on poverty and improving conditions for Negroes while their own needs were being ignored. . . . Thus the votes that Wallace picked up from young workers cannot be attributed to racism pure and simple. They must also be seen, at least in part, as an expression of rebellion— a misguided rebellion, to be sure—against the circumstances of relative economic insecurity.

Only when labor leadership impugned Wallace's record of support for the workingman's cause did he begin to lose support, primarily to Humphrey.

What is striking about the frustrations of the young white working class is the similarity they bear to those of their college cousins. Both are expressing feelings of powerlessness, of being unable to control the fast-changing world around them. As the college student reacts to the alienating effect of the large and impersonal university, so the young worker strikes out at the degradation which he experiences at the hands of the corporate bureaucracy. In this regard, it is noteworthy that the most alienated young workers, if the Wallace vote may be taken as an index of alienation, are union members, indicating employment in the larger industrial establishments. The union no longer serves as a dis-alienating factor. Tom Kahn calls the young worker an "invisible youth" and describes him as a man with "a lack of identification with, and appreciation for, the past struggles and achievements of the labor movement. These struggles and achievements were won before the young worker entered the labor market and he cannot see how his life was transformed by his union. For him, the union is simply an instrument for winning periodic wage hikes and even in this he may feel it is not doing a good enough job."

When the frustrated young worker rebels, he is likely to lash out at convenient symbols of his frustration—in particular, blacks and students who appear to be evil harbingers of change.

Thus the root causes of unrest, frustration, and powerlessness are the same for both student and young worker, but their positions in society have determined that they shall be set as opposing forces. It often seems that the reactions of both groups may be compared to that of the Scottish miner who, returning from the mines one day, informed his wife that he was on strike. "What for?" she asked. "I don't know," he replied, "but I'm not going back till we get it."

In this age of violent protests, one cannot expect that the young workers will remain quiescent much longer. Their revolt, justifying itself in the very rhetoric and devices employed by young blacks and students—the most immediate objects of young workers' antagonism—could be exceedingly disruptive. Whereas student disorders have been primarily limited to the isolated university community, similar hostility expressed by young workers and directed at the students, the blacks, the government, or even their own unions, could severely upset the national economy. The specter of a young workers' revolt is raised not to frighten, but to show the necessity of dealing with the legitimate claims of this very large segment of society.

WHAT MUST BE DONE

Responsibility for meeting the material and psychological needs of young workers rests with the media, the schools, business management, unions, and the government.

The mass media should take care, as they are beginning to do with blacks, to divest themselves of the prejudices of the educated middle class when reporting about the working-class young. Moreover, greater attention should be given to this group's problems, outlook, and aspirations. Artists and writers have a responsibility here, too.

The Kerner Commission recommended the establishment of an Institute of Urban Communications which would have as its central purpose the improvement of the relations of the media with the black community. Such a body might also be useful as a means of reviewing media coverage of the white working-class point of view. Much of the white working-class is highly ethnicized—the melting-pot theory notwithstanding. A television series describing the continuing traditions of America's transplanted Lithuanian, Irish, Italian, Greek, and other minorities—perhaps something along the lines of Bill Cosby's narration of the black history series —would be welcome.

Similarly, the academic community must give more attention to the place of the worker in society. While new departments are being established at many universities to examine the black man's place in society, only one course dealing with white working-class values, "Labor and Society" at New York University, is offered for sociology students anywhere in the country. Union officials should be invited to discuss the content of such a course. Local working-class citizens and representatives of ethnic groups might be asked to speak on what they see as their role in the community, and their view of the type of society and working environment they are striving for. The important point is that middle-class students learn to respect the viewpoint of the man who, in writer Jimmy Breslin's words, "lives above the drugstore." Just as the student has rebelled against racial discrimination, so he should be wary of economic and class discrimination. The light of academic and intellectual objectivity must illumine this darkness too.

Businesses can help ameliorate the sense of alienation among employees by adopting labor practices which give the employee greater control over his working environment. For example, the Harwood Manufacturing Company, a Virginia concern making wearing apparel, has experimented successfully with allowing employees to decide their own work procedures. Management is there only in a consulting relationship. As a result of true sharing of responsibilities, annual employee turnover has been reduced from 18 percent to 4 percent, and absenteeism has dropped from 17 percent to 4 percent. Another company, Non-Linear Systems, converted from assembly-line production to a system in which the entire product is made by a single employee (the company christened itself after its new production method). Despite the storied glories of specialization, man-hours required to complete a product dropped by 50 percent. In another company, management told employees to draw up their own salary schedules, a rather radical innovation that at first met resistance but later enthusiasm from everyone.

The unions too must assume responsibility for helping young workers overcome their sense of alienation. Efforts should be directed at easing the financial plight of the young married worker and giving him a better sense of participation in union affairs.

One-half of all union members are less than forty years of age. This seems anomalous when compared to the mean age of organized labor's leadership hierarchy. The International Labor Organization (ILO), representing trade unionists from all over the globe, recognizes this inconsistency and has called for the establishment of "youth wings" as formal adjuncts on union organization charts. The AFL-CIO, however, has rebuffed this recommendation. In the October, 1969, issue of *The American Federationist,* Walker G. Davis, director of the AFL-CIO Department of Education, wrote: "Rather than treat young trade unionists in a separatist way, it would seem to be more creditable and productive to engage them in the activities of a wide range of existing union programs such as collective bargaining workshops, organizing conferences, community services and political action. Hence, the means to involve and invite them into the trade union and community mainstream are already available at the local union, international union, central body and federation levels." Davis does not mention a greater role for the young trade unionist within the political structure of the union. Perhaps that is implicit in his remarks; however, because political powerlessness is one of the causes of current unrest, the proposed changes ought to be carefully spelled out. Why not state in the union constitution that the executive council or other governing body is to have representation from all age groups in the union proportionate to their numbers?

Unions probably could reach agreements with management to provide for special advancement and the equivalent of seniority privileges for young workers with superior educational backgrounds. Some unions have pioneered in that direction already. The educational attainment of most workers, according to 1968 figures, is still low, with an average of 9.8 years of schooling for

menial laborers to 12.6 years for sales workers. When a man has special technical training before he enters the work force, it would seem appropriate to reduce his apprentice period or even allow him to advance directly to a foreman position.

Finally, the federal government, under the leadership of the President, should make the concerns of the young working man and his family its concern too. Present efforts, spurred by Housing and Urban Development Secretary George Romney, to construct inexpensive housing through new assembly-line techniques and prefabrication will be of direct help to young workers in the better-paying jobs. And, if acted upon, plans to remove the working poor from the income tax rolls will benefit young workers in less well-paying jobs. These initiatives deserve support.

In addition, the government should help relax the economic squeeze on young workers by providing long-term loans for major expenditures. These loans would require only small payments during the difficult early years of a person's working career, leaving the heaviest payments until later in life when his children are grown up and his income higher. One obvious source for such loans would be the FHA, since the biggest expenditure a young worker faces is housing and since a high percentage of young working men are military veterans. It seems only fair that veterans who do not take advantage of the GI Bill to get advanced education should be rewarded for their service in some other fashion.

Other programs and policies should also be considered. Tax relief for education costs is one possibility. Raising the minimum income level—now set at $6,900—at which families may deduct child-care expenses from their income tax would permit more wives to hold that ofttimes vital second job. A children's allowance, similar to the subsidies paid to families in most other industrial nations, ought to be looked at as a possible means of alleviating economic hardship. Increased federal support for child-care facilities for non-poverty working-class families would permit many more wives to work and would enable families to shoulder their own economic burdens.

No single program, however, is going to curb the growing alienation of the young working man from his society. It will take action on all the fronts we have mentioned. It behooves the President not only to act through the government, but to prod the nation's labor, business, educational, and communications leadership to give this important and neglected segment of our population a more respectful hearing. For the youth revolt is not confined to the campus or the ghetto; it exists wherever young people find their legitimate needs neglected. And the young laborer is no exception.

Chapter 5

YOUTH AND BUSINESS

Who Will Man Free Enterprise?

"If industry is going to answer questions such as why don't kids want to work for us, why do bright kids decline job offers, why do kids come to us with a chip on their shoulders, industry is going to have to retrain the thinking of its leadership group. Management must learn how to listen. . . . Industry is going to experience change. The whole test of our society is whether we can accommodate."[1]

These remarks by Dean William Haber of the University of Michigan illuminate one of the most significant attitudes among young people toward American society—their dissatisfaction with the business world. Although the young men and women who choose careers in business are by no means radical in their outlook, many of the most talented and thoughtful among them believe that there is much in the corporate world that needs to be put in order. For, unlike the previous generation, who believed that, as Calvin Coolidge put it, "The business of America is business," today's youth are more apt to feel that the business of business should be America.

Symptoms of this widespread discontent are rife:

According to an editor of *Fortune* magazine: "The recent much-heralded increase in executive turnover is mostly explained by the restlessness of young executives, and there is no reason to believe that this restlessness will diminish."[2]

A Research Institute of America poll of young Americans revealed that only 7 percent thought that business had made "the most significant contribution to the cause of a better life in America for all."[3]

54

A *Fortune*-sponsored poll found that most young people do not welcome more emphasis on private enterprise in society, and that business and related careers were the choice of less than 20 percent of college students.[4]

In 1966 more Harvard seniors opted for the Peace Corps than for careers in business; and only 6 percent of the Class of 1968 went directly into business.[5]

Why are business careers far less attractive to bright young people than they used to be? Perhaps Norman Mailer summed up the problem most succinctly:

> The authority had operated on [youth's] brain with commercials, and washed their brain with packaged education, packaged politics. The authority had presented itself as honorable, and it was corrupt, corrupt as payola on television, and scandals concerning the safety of automobiles, and scandals concerning the leasing of aviation contracts—the real scandals as everyone was beginning to sense were more intimate and could be found in all the products in all the suburban homes which did not work so well as they should have worked, and broke down too soon for mysterious reasons. The shoddiness was buried in the package, buried somewhere in the undiscoverable root of all those modern factories with their sanitized aisles and automated machines; perhaps one place the shoddiness was buried was in the hangovers of a working class finally alienated from any remote interest or attention in the process of the work itself. Work was shoddy everywhere. Even in the Warren Commission.
>
> Finally, this new generation of the Left hated the authority, because the authority lied. It lied through the teeth of corporation executives as Cabinet officials and police enforcement officers and newspaper editors and advertising agencies, and in its mass magazines, where the subtlest apologies for the disasters of the authority (and the neatest deformations of the news) were grafted in the best possible style into the ever-open mind of the walking American lobotomy: the corporation office worker and his high school son.[6]

Perhaps the best statement by a young person on the attitude of youth toward business was that of a California student leader: "I think there are two good reasons why I don't want to be a business man: first I don't think the job would let me exercise my brain enough to keep it from going sour, and second, I couldn't respect any organization that had a one-track mind about making a profit."

Almost all the opposition that young people express against business can be boiled down to two basic issues—challenge and social responsibility.

The Challenge of a Business Career

Among the arguments decrying the lack of opportunity for individual creativity in a business career, we might enumerate the following:

That the business hierarchy is too highly structured and promotions are too often based on length of service rather than performance.

That resistance to change is so deeply ingrained that new methods of operation are dismissed without trial, even when these methods have had demonstrable success elsewhere.

That jobs are too rigidly codified, with too many details to occupy one's mind. The amount of red tape is staggering.

That makework, undue specialization, and overlapping duties keep everyone working inefficiently.

That above all, creativity is stifled. The president of IBM once designed a wall plaque with the simple imperative THINK, but young people doubt that the message has gotten through to most businessmen.

All these complaints add up to one basic grievance, stated by an economics student at the University of Iowa: "If I take a job in business, I lose my ability to control my environment. I become a pawn in somebody else's chess game, and maybe if I stick it out for thirty years I'll get to be a more important piece, but I'll never get to the point where I'm playing my own game." In short, young people will no longer be satisfied with just money from their business careers; they want a creative experience as well.

Of course, the business world is not confined to the large corporations. Many young people with unusual entrepreneurial acumen have become successful in their own enterprises. The entertainment industry has proved particularly hospitable to the young. The younger the individual, the better he will understand what will "sell" to the youth culture. And so we have seen an avalanche of rock groups, managers, and agents who are far younger than the average age in the music trade. Others have been able to transform their understanding of the special interests of young people into original and lucrative enterprises: Commercial artist Peter Max and designer Betsey Johnson are examples.

Clearly, however, most bright young people will not have the opportunity to launch their own enterprise at age twenty-five. The vast majority will find themselves employed in firms run by older people, especially large corporations. How can they fulfill their creative potential in the corporate bureaucracy?

For those with some scientific or inventive expertise, the problem is not serious. A government advisory commission on technology and innovation reported that a remarkable percentage of modern inventions still come from individuals rather than research teams. Many technologically oriented companies now realize that genius can best be fostered by giving the individual the opportunity to set his own objectives and his own course. To the unsuspecting individual coming from the button-down, crew-cut world of the conventional corporation, a visit to a modern technological firm such as a computer software company can be a real eye-opener: Beards, Levi's, and long hair abound, but more important, so do creative minds.

But what about the young person who has not specialized in the sciences? Corporations will soon be flooded with managerial talent from the post–World War II generation. Consider the projections of a DuPont economist: Because of the low birth rates during the 1930s and early 1940s and the birth explosion in the late 1940s and 1950s, by 1975 the age group 15–29 will outnumber the age group 30–44 by 57 percent![7] For business executives, this means that lower and middle managerial posts will be filled by younger and younger employees. And if they demand more meaningful jobs, more meaningful jobs will have to be devised.

One way in which many firms have solved this problem is to make younger executives division or field managers. These individuals are generally given broad leeway in running their offices, taking responsibility for policy, hiring, and innovating systems. Nor does this freedom compromise the effectiveness of the whole organization. "Any industrial manager who does not understand the great value of the nonconformist attitudes of this student generation to business is in trouble," states an oil-company recruiter. "We don't care whether they wear beards and long hair. It's what's inside them that counts." [8] This attitude of liberality toward youth will benefit the corporation itself in the long run.

Finally, the broadening of opportunities for bright young employees can only benefit all employees. It is no secret that inefficiency can often be traced to boredom; young, creative management can stimulate employees to better efforts and hence greater job satisfaction.

Some businesses are participating in programs to give middle-level executives a broader perspective and more general satisfaction in their work, by encouraging them to take part in community affairs or continue their formal education. Programs such as the University of Pennsylvania's Humanistic Studies for Executives are designed with this in mind. Why not encourage businessmen to take courses with full-time students, to facilitate communication between these age groups?

SOCIAL RESPONSIBILITY

A young Delaware journalist recently summed up the complaints in this area: "We look longingly at the tremendous potential of business to do good for society, but we see no one turning to put that potential to use—unless forced to by public pressure." [9]

Examples of this abound:

The content of the typical annual report published by any publicly held corporation is limited to the issue of profit and return on the stockholder's investment; there is no word about how company policy affects employees, customers, and the general public.

A large aviation company held a management seminar where a presentation was made of the need for research and technology to be tied to the whole range of human aspirations. After the speaker was through, a vice president asked, "This is all very interesting, but how will it sell airplanes?"

Waste created by a Boston power company had been darkening the skies for so many years that Boston University students awarded the firm a mock prize for pollution.

Manufacturers, especially paper manufacturers, have contributed greatly to water pollution.

Thousands of citizens around the country are being deafened by the noise pollution created by jet planes.

Land-development companies are found everywhere busily building the slums of the 1970s.

Auto manufacturers have responded sluggishly, at best, to evidence of safety hazards built into cars.

Price-fixing scandals remain with us, as do shoddy merchandise, planned obsolescence, and fraudulent advertising.

All these issues of social responsibility weigh heavily on the minds of idealistic youth, and very often it is a corporation that is cast in the role of the villain. Such an image hardly serves as a good recruiting tool. If business wants to attract top young talent—and keep such talent happy—it must not only identify itself with a socially responsible, humanitarian "image," but also lend substance to that image; and it must take a stand on public questions.

The pendulum of involvement has swung far away from the self-interested political manipulations of the nineteenth-century "robber barons": Today many businesses seem to feel that they have no social or political role at all—indeed, no role other than to sell their product. But other institutions, notably churches and universities, are groping for a political role. They know that they cannot ignore the world around them, or the effects their policies have on that world—and businesses should follow suit. A factory or law firm has not satisfied its obligation to the community by providing jobs; it must also help the community channel its growth in constructive, people-centered ways.

Business should not abandon the profit motive as the basic element in its decision making. But within this framework, it must develop—and schedule funds for—long-range concern for the society and the environment within which it operates.

Many business firms have already begun to perceive their responsibility to community and nation. The examples below demonstrate just a few of the ways in which businesses are serving the public—and themselves:

The National Alliance of Businessmen was established in 1968 to attack the problem of hard-core unemployment. The business community recognized its stake in full utilization of the nation's human resources. The NAB set as its goal the training of 100,000 hard-core unemployed by June, 1969, and 500,000 by June, 1971, The earlier quota was exceeded months in advance, thanks to the extensive efforts of such corporate giants as Lockheed Aircraft and General Electric. These firms have recruited and trained thousands of men and women who just a few years ago were not considered worth the trouble.

Some corporations have gone to the heart of the same problem by locating plants in ghetto areas where unemployment is highest and work skills lowest. AVCO Corporation found that the move to the Boston ghetto of Roxbury was expensive, but the problems it encountered and the solutions it developed have served as an education to the entire business community.

Aerojet-General Corporation made a similar commitment to its community by establishing a subsidiary in the Watts section of Los Angeles. The subsidiary manufactures tents, a far cry from the company's standard product line, but it does make money, and more important, it provides jobs and training to the community.

After the 1967 Detroit riots, the Ford Motor Company set up job-recruitment centers in the ghetto. The company abolished employment tests and the requirement for a "clean" police record as an absolute prerequisite for obtaining a job.

Business has also attacked the problem of low-income housing. The insurance industry has received public acclaim for its offer to make available a billion dollars for investment in ghetto areas. Other firms have concentrated on rehabilitation of substandard housing, and both U.S. Gypsum and National Gypsum have conducted extensive programs in many disadvantaged areas. These firms have issued public statements that they are available for consultation with anyone interested in this activity.

The profit motive has led many firms to attack the pressing social needs of our environment. For example, the Budd Company has spent millions in the development of a new high-speed commuter train that should help alleviate the transportation bottleneck.

Several companies are competing for contracts to provide the equipment for the treatment of water utilized in industrial processes; another group is devising methods to combat air pollution.

Several forest-products companies are opening up their forest lands to the public; this, of course, will increase the return on their assets, but it will also help alleviate the need for recreational facilities.

The Rouse Company, a real-estate development concern, has built Columbia, Maryland, a planned city which some day may house 100,000 people in a complete living environment. Not only has this city helped to improve the Baltimore-Washington economic region, but it serves as a prototype of the "new town" which could have a very beneficial impact on our national growth.

A number of firms have arisen that run children's day-care centers on a franchise basis.

In short, it has become good business to second-guess the needs of society. This type of creative and socially responsible thinking in American business might prove to be a rallying point for today's alienated youth.

Young people *should* prod the social conscience of the business community, and this challenge can be met in ways that may not only bring about a reconciliation of differences, but will also speed up the process of beneficial social change.

Indeed, in some cases reconciliation has already begun. Dialogues among business leaders, concerned youths, and government officials are taking place. Out of these programs can come an easing of youthful frustration at being ignored, as well as many important suggestions, such as fresh insights into pollution control and the problem of hard-core unemployment, and better understanding of what the younger generation wants in the way of protective legislation.

THE LEGAL PROFESSION

The legal profession, like business, is one in which young people are suspicious of the large firm, where, they feel, there is a lack of social responsibility and little opportunity for meaningful work. Like business schools, law schools are turning out more and more graduates who refuse to follow the well-trodden paths to success. A former president of Brandeis University, himself an attorney, estimates that 25 to 30 percent of law students in the best schools have no intention of practicing law.[10]

The new social awareness among students has revolutionized law schools. For example:

New courses are given, such as "Race, Racism, and American Law" (Harvard), "Law for the Poor in an Affluent Society" (Columbia), "Consumer Protection" (Stanford), "Natural Resources" (University of California), and "Urban Public School Systems" (University of Chicago).[11]

Schools like Stanford and Harvard are stressing clinical field work, including student-run legal-aid bureaus, as part of their law curricula.

Law schools are working with social science departments in an effort to make the study of law more "relevant." These related fields include economics, business, political science, and psychiatry.

Brandeis is pioneering a new type of law school, aimed specifically at training government policy-makers.[12]

A survey by the Cornell Law School reveals that about one out of four law students in this country will be taking courses in environmental law in the 1970–71 school year.[13]

Moreover, lawyers are turning away from the prestigious Wall Street firms and lending their talents to legal-aid bureaus, Office of Opportunity poverty casework, draft cases, and government. In New York and Chicago young lawyers live in communes and defend black militants and student protesters and fight laws against abortion, marijuana use, and obscenity. In San Francisco young attorneys stopped a federal urban-renewal project that was deemed injurious to people's rights. In Nashville a young lawyer organized a neighborhood into a successful anti-pollution group. Even on Wall Street and in well-heeled Washington firms, younger recruits are allowed to devote time (as much as one month a year) to social action work.[14] And each summer a number of law students turn down lucrative jobs to volunteer their services to Ralph Nader.

No doubt in the future we will see many more public crusaders like Nader, for the law profession, like business, has already begun to feel the impact of the idealism of today's youth.

THE ROLE OF GOVERNMENT

There is much that can be done by government to improve relations between the young and the business community. The following are several of the best ideas which have been advocated in campus newspapers, the underground press, and other forums for youth:

Limitations on campaign spending. Many young people see legislators as pawns of the businessmen who contribute heavily to their campaigns. They feel that many politicians are so dependent at re-election time on campaign dollars that they must pander to special-interest groups lest they find their campaign coffers empty. If there were strict limits on the amount of money that could be spent in a campaign, there would be less likelihood that a candidate could be compromised; he would be beholden only to the people. Any reduction in campaign spending might be offset by some type of indirect public subsidy, such as free air time. The spiraling costs of running for office determine to a large degree the type of person who runs, and this is wrong.

Accountability of public officials. In an era when even the most highly respected members of government—Supreme Court justices and United States Senators—are sometimes revealed to have engaged in questionable relationships with the business community, young and old people alike become cynical about the coziness between government and business. There should be stricter controls on lobbying activities, and more emphasis on self-policing of legislative bodies. A public revelation of all sources of income should be required of all men in high office—national, state, and local.

Consumer protection. The administration should be diligent in its regulation of business practices, for the excesses of one industry can poison the reputation of business as a whole. Every defective car recalled by Detroit, every beach spoiled by irresponsible oil drillers, every industrialist caught price fixing, increases the alienation of young people from business. We need tougher laws against such malpractices, tougher restrictions on billboards on highways, higher rates for "junk mail," and closer controls on the claims of advertising and packaging. This also means fast and convenient recourses for consumers whose purchases have failed to live up to advertised specifications. It means, above all, stringent anti-pollution controls to protect against all types of environmental destruction.

Incentives to social action. Government can offer tax and other incentives for business to become more responsive to the social needs of the nation. Such incentives might include guarantees or insurance that would lower the cost of borrowed capital, just as Federal National Mortgage Association mortgages make money available to borrowers. They might include a reordering of the investment tax credit (which stimulated widespread capital spending in the early 1960s) that would favor businesses with social-service aspects. Government agencies issuing contracts should show special preferences to businesses that demonstrate social concern (such as training programs for minority groups) in their operations. Public recognition should be given any business that has shown outstanding responsibility for social reform.

Free enterprise in service to the people. The government should help business toward a constructive role in society by relinquishing the functions of many government services to the private sector. There is great reason for confidence in the free-enterprise system and in the efficiency of the modern corporation. Such efficiency is sorely lacking in such government services as the welfare agencies and the post office. Businesses, guided by the profit motive and competing for contracts to handle specific public functions and management of certain local government units, can offer fresh approaches to the problem of declining quality in government services.

Businesses should be given tax breaks to encourage the development of new towns. Any corporation or group of corporations that could offer enough jobs to support 1,000 households would be encouraged to negotiate with the federal government for a franchise to develop a new town, at a location agreed upon by federal planning agencies and the corporate planning staff. The franchise would give the corporation the right to develop a master plan for the total environment of that community—similar to the plans developed at Reston, Virginia, or Columbia, Maryland. Recreation, water, power, law enforcement, and city government would be included in the scope of the plan, and the corporation would also be given a free hand to develop the area peripheral to the original territory (consistent with good conservation principles).

Of course, business leadership in the inner city, along the lines of the Urban Coalition or New York's Bedford-Stuyvesant Corporation, should also be encouraged.

To Renew Free Enterprise

American business—within the free-enterprise system, subject to government regulation and public scrutiny, and spurred by the administration—can recover the central place it once held in the aspirations of American youth. The free-enterprise system remains the nation's best hope for economic growth. If business addresses itself to the nation's hope for social reform and individual self-fulfillment, then it will find all the young talent it needs. The inspiration of youthful idealism can transform the whole economic system to serve the goals of *all* Americans.

Chapter 6

THE MILITARY

Justice for the Soldier

Few issues have been as prominent in the ferment of youth over the past five years as the role of the military. When one out of every five men aged eighteen to twenty-four is in uniform, it is small wonder that the question of one's military "obligation" looms large in any discussion of the discontents of young people.

There is a problem in discussing the military here, because it is also connected with so many political issues not restricted to the interests of the soldier: the war in Vietnam, military expenditures, the military influence in society, militarization of foreign policy, wartime atrocities, and so on. All of these topics concern all of us as citizens, but because they do not especially affect soldiers—mostly young men—they will not be discussed below.

There is another topic, of momentous importance to young people, that also will go undiscussed here except for a brief note. That is the question of the draft and the volunteer army. In 1966 The Ripon Society proposed eliminating the draft, raising salaries and other emoluments of a military career, and establishing a 2.7-million-man volunteer army.[1] Others in the Republican party proposed the same kind of basic reform around that time,[2] and President Nixon made it one of his programs. The debate about the volunteer army is vitally important, but since it has already engaged the public's attention (with, we must note, popular approval for the idea),[3] we shall move on to other issues facing the man in uniform.

We shall not overly concern ourselves with issues relating to a nation at war, because we look forward to peace in the near future.

We shall address ourselves to problems that arise in the military even in peacetime (recognizing also that even in time of war, most soldiers are not on the battlefield).

A New Generation in Uniform

With the enormous rise in the draft since the escalation in Vietnam, the military has absorbed many thousands of young people who never intended to wear olive drab. First sergeants find themselves face to face with young men who are part of the generational constituency described in the first part of this book. Their desires, their goals, their values are often diametrically opposed to those of the military establishment, and this has created many problems for the service.

Nor will these problems disappear when draft calls diminish. If, as appears inevitable, the army will rely upon voluntary enlistments in the future, it is essential that the military life be made more appealing to young people. There are potent reasons why some young men could find enlistment in their own best interests. For the economically deprived, the military can provide job skills and economic security; for the ethnically discriminated against, the military is more of an equal-opportunity employer than most private institutions. But if the economically and ethnically disadvantaged young are "turned off" by the idiosyncrasies of the military life, these advantages will be outweighed.

There are many ways, costing nothing but of great symbolic significance, in which officers and non-commissioned officers (NCOs) can make life more attractive to recruits. It goes without saying that many of the arbitrary and petty day-to-day rules and events of military life could be changed without great damage to discipline and with great benefit to morale.

The military originally adopted haircut regulations for sanitary purposes; today they have been elevated to a dogma among officers who conduct daily inspections to make certain that no hair dares touch cheek or nape. Surely with sanitary conditions as they are today, there is no reason why men who leave the post should be made to feel like freaks among their sideburned contemporaries. There would be no loss of discipline if these pointless regulations were junked, and the boost to morale would be enormous. Hair length is an especially sensitive issue among black soldiers, who see their civilian peers sporting Afros to proclaim their ethnic pride. In this age of black aspirations, such restrictions help to create racial tensions, which have erupted in bloodshed at some bases.

A more serious cause of racial tension is the attitude of so many officers and NCOs, many of whom hail from the rural South, where whites are hardly known for racial toleration. One soldier wrote home from Vietnam:

> Unfortunately, the army seems to tolerate all too well various expressions of race prejudice, tribal bigotry, and biased opinions of other cultures and ideologies. The typical army indoctrination course could make some effort to root out these preconceived half-truths and untruths, but, unfortunately, the army seems so obsessed with teaching anti-Communism in the courses that they reinforce these provincial bigotries rather than eradicate them. One only has to listen attentively to an average barracks conversation to realize that the ordinary recruit equates in his mind "stinking gooks, Jews, foreigners, and Communists." [4]

These problems, so similar to ethnic problems in civilian society, will not be solved by official pronouncements and changes in regulations alone. To a great extent, they are the result of a class of officers and NCOs insensitive to the reasonable desires of young recruits. Perhaps only when the present generation of officers and NCOs is replaced will conditions change significantly.

But until change does occur, the military will find it increasingly difficult to attract the kind of talent it wants. It is time for the military to take a good hard look at itself and reassess its discipline and indoctrination procedures.

REFORMING THE LEGAL CODE

One major area in which basic reform can be instituted by act of Congress is military law. Despite the improvements made in the system in 1968, there is a long way to go toward ensuring maximum justice within a military context.

There are at least two areas of military justice where major reforms would be helpful and several other places where specific changes in present procedures should be implemented. Before discussing these changes, however, it is important to underscore that they must be evaluated in the light of two special problems of military as compared to civilian justice.

First, the system of military justice necessarily involves more coercion than the civilian system. Most servicemen are not voluntarily in the service—they have either enlisted under pressure or been drafted. This coercion factor will be reduced as the nation moves toward a volunteer army. However, the requirements of coercion in military discipline will probably never be reduced. Whereas in civilian society only the extremes of behavior are regulated by the judicial system, in the military the requirements must be much more restrictive—and thus the problems of military justice are more difficult to resolve.

Second, military justice cannot assume that everyone is playing by the same rules; the enemy cannot be compelled to play by the rules. Thus, especially in a combat context, the problems of military justice are significantly different from the problems of civilian justice.

Keeping these two caveats clearly in mind, we can now consider some major steps that would improve military justice.

COMMAND INFLUENCE

Picture yourself as a lawyer, a captain in the Army. You have just been appointed to defend an enlisted man at a court-martial because of a determination by your superior officer that the man has committed an offense under such circumstances that he deserves to be tried before the military's most severe tribunal. You begin your investigation and find that your client was not really absent without official leave (AWOL), but rather that your superior messed up his orders and in effect left him unassigned for almost a year. But then you think, If I bring all this up at the trial, it might get the old man mad. After all, I'll have to state for public record that he made a stupid blunder. I wonder what my next efficiency report will look like. I'd really like to make major. . . .

Under the Uniform Code of Military Justice (10 U.S.C.A. Chap.

47), the convening authority, usually the commanding officer of the base or ship, makes a decision whether to convene a court-martial, to bring the "offender" before an administrative board (thereby avoiding the requirements of the Uniform Code of Military Justice), or to ignore the offense. If he chooses to convene a court-martial, he decides whether to convene a general, special, or summary court (in decreasing order of severity), and then appoints not only the members of the court, but also the lawyers *for both sides,* usually from his own command. Think about that. If you were accused, would you want your accuser to appoint your judge, jury, and attorney—*and to outrank and command them all?* In the words of former Senator Joseph Tydings, of Maryland: "This arrangement whereby the defense counsel is under the control of a military officer who is likened to a prosecuting attorney is clearly at odds with the basic philosophy of our adversary system of justice."[5] So too is there a problem with the members of the court, who are appointed by the convening authority.

Article 37 of the UCMJ makes command influence unlawful, but this article is widely thought to be ineffectual. The American Veterans Committee maintains that "the independence of the military justice system continues to be prejudiced by the threat of command influence, notwithstanding article 37 of the code."[6] The Supreme Court in *O'Callahan vs. Parker* (1969) said that the problem "is a pervasive one in military law, despite strenuous efforts to eliminate the danger." According to Professor Joseph W. Bishop, Jr., of the Yale Law School, "illegal command influence is often intangible and hard to find in the record."[7]

The urgency of the problem is highlighted in a statement by the American Legion: "The court's primary purpose is to administer justice and not carry out the mandates and desires of a commanding officer. *Any other concept will render the elaborate protection of the accused mere pretentions and idle gestures*" [italics added].[8]

This situation cannot be tolerated. But the services do not defend themselves against charges of command influence on the grounds of military efficiency or the like; *they deny its existence.* In the words of Brigadier General Kenneth J. Hodson, Assistant Judge Advocate General of the Army, "Certainly in the Army the convening authority can select the court and still have the court free, independent, and impartial to exercise its own judgment." [9]

General Hodson also stated on this subject: "Most officers in the Army are familiar with acting independently and with performing independently, and they carry out the duties of court just as they carry out their other duties, without fear of reprisal, and completely independently and impartially . . ." [10]

Rear Admiral Wilfred A. Hearn, Judge Advocate General of the Navy, had this to say: "I am not aware of any instance in the Navy where the court membership coming from the command or convening authority has had any effect whatsoever upon the outcome of the case." [11]

Major General R. W. Manss, Judge Advocate General of the Air Force, stated in 1966, "I know we have, in the Air Force, pretty well gotten our commanders convinced that command influence is a bad thing, and this starts right at the top, and works all the way down, and is an educational proposition." [12]

Are you convinced? Consider these remarks of Senator Tydings: "So long as the court-martial system continues to operate along command lines and in an atmosphere of command control, court-martial personnel will remain sensitive to the practical realities of military life." [13]

The following procedural revisions would be beneficial in relieving the threat of command influence:

Removing selection of defense counsel from the control of the military commander who convenes a court-martial.

Appointing an independent military trial command to select defense counsel, so that command influence cannot adversely affect the fairness of the proceedings.

Removing selection of jury members from the control of the military commander who convenes a court-martial and transferring it to an independent trial command.

Requiring that the presiding officer at an Article 32 pre-trial investigation be an independent, qualified legal officer rather than a non-lawyer from the immediate command of the convening authority.

Defining the type of court-martial by the possible sentence rather than leaving the decision to the discretion of the convening authority and thus allowing him to indicate by his choice his impression of the severity of the offense.

Selection of defense counsel. This could well be the most important single change. A truly independent defense lawyer can often bring facts to bear which will expose command influence and bring justice to his client. Unfortunately, this sometimes requires him to uncover mistakes of officers who are his direct superiors, placing him in an incredible conflict-of-interest bind: Either he pleads his client's case vigorously and risks subtle but certain retaliation for frustrating the wishes of the convening authority and the Staff Judge Advocate (his superiors) who sent his client to trial, or he must fail to fulfill his moral and legal duty as defense counsel.

Only complete independence between defense counsel and the command convening the court-martial can allow full and vigorous argument on behalf of the accused—and we can settle for no less if we are to achieve true justice in the military. Recent interviews indicate that this conflict-of-interest problem has persisted even after passage of the Military Justice Act of 1968, which deprived the convening authority of the power to evaluate defense counsel for personnel files, although still allowing him to appoint defense counsel; they suggest that it is essential for defense counsel to be as independent as the military judges. (See S.3117 introduced in the Senate on November 5, 1969, by Senator Tydings.)

Selection of jury members. Many of the same arguments for an independent defense counsel are applicable to the question of an independent jury. Where an officer's superior decides to send a case to trial, especially before a full general court-martial, that officer can assume that his commander at least entertains the thought that the man is guilty of a serious offense and might expect the court to decide accordingly. Further, the convening authority might intentionally or even unconsciously select for jury duty members of his command whom he thinks will share his views on the particular offense. In neither case is the accused tried before an impartial jury. In the words of Senator Tydings, "This system of court member selection which practically invites abuse is as inimical to the appearance of judicial impartiality as an actual showing of abuse." [14]

The Article 32 officer. Before a case can be referred to a general court-martial, an investigation is required by Article 32 of the UCMJ, much like the civilian grand-jury system. As presently structured, however, this "investigation" can be a farce. Picture the hearing room: At the center table sits the presiding officer, an infantry captain with no legal experience, possibly in his first exposure to the workings of the legal system. On the left sit an Army captain, a qualified legal officer from the office of the Staff Judge Advocate, a civilian attorney also representing the accused, and the accused himself. On the right sits no one. The convening authority has recommended a general court-martial, but he is not represented. Only the charge sheets represent the prosecution. Clearly nervous and apologetic, the presiding officer reads to the accused each word of each charge, each word of the requisite articles of the code and regulations advising the accused of his rights, fills out his various forms, and the "investigation" is about to begin in earnest.

First, the defense attorneys object to the admissibility of some of the documents necessary to the charges, for instance the morning reports that indicate absence, which are necessary to the charge of absence without official leave (AWOL). The presiding officer is stymied; he has never read anything about rules of evidence. Next, the defense attorneys offer a defense to the charge; for instance, there might be documents indicating that the accused was in fact on leave or even discharged from the service at the date of his alleged offense. The presiding officer, struggling with legal concepts such as "burden of proof," "affirmative defense," and various "presumptions," repeatedly requests the defense attorneys to repeat their statements slowly, often with a request for an explanation, so that he may write them down (there is no stenographer).

After several more acts in this confusing drama, the presiding officer leaves with his papers and notes and faces two tasks: He must summarize an "investigation" that he does not understand, and he must recommend the appropriate next step, whether it be a general, special, or summary court-martial, an administrative proceeding, or dropping the whole matter. Wishing that he had law-school training, he laboriously prepares the report of the investigation and makes his recommendation, a special court-martial rather than the general court-martial recommended by the convening authority on the advice of his lawyer, the Staff Judge Advocate. The presiding officer's report does not go directly to the convening authority, however; it goes to the Staff Judge Advocate (who recommended the general court-martial in the first place). Being a trained legal officer, the Judge Advocate can easily consider his legal training as justification for reversing any recommendation from the presiding officer, and may even reinstate the recommendation of a general court-martial. The muddled summary of the "investigation" and the recommendations for proceeding then reach the desk of the convening authority, often a general without any legal training. From this confused summary record of an investigation conducted by a legal amateur, another legal amateur must make a legal decision about how to proceed. Since his own lawyer (the Staff Judge Advocate) has recommended a general court-martial, the result of this confusion is likely to be a reaffirmation of the convening authority's own previous decision—general court-martial.

What purpose did the whole Article 32 investigative procedure serve? Can the accused be said to have in any way benefited from having his civilian and military counsel argue sophisticated points of law to a man untutored in the law who is going to summarize the record without a transcript for review by the man who made the original recommendation for a general court-martial? The author, having participated in just such a case, cannot conceive how such a proceeding could fulfill the intent of Congress in enacting Article 32.

Further, the inefficiency of such a procedure is extreme. Because an Article 32 investigation is not presided over by a legal officer, command influence is almost inevitable; also, an erroneous decision to uphold the original recommendation of a general court-martial requires additional time of defense attorneys, requires the time of a military judge (a legal officer) and five officers as court members, and the time of prosecuting attorneys as well, most of which would have been unnecessary had the Article 32 investigation produced a proper result.

But beyond inefficiency, the very fact that so many high-priced men are assembled to deal with the offense gives it an air of severity. These officers on the court, not accustomed to spending large amounts of time on trivial matters and not specially trained in principles of jurisprudence, must be psychologically affected by the overkill of the machinery of military justice upon which the commanding officer can call when he wishes.

Professor Seymour W. Wurfel, of the University of North Carolina, has pointed out: "As presently conducted Article 32 investigations consume officer time. Practically all errors made at that critical stage of the proceedings result from lay ignorance and not from any attempt to overreach the accused. It would be no more costly and much more effective if Article 32 time is expended by lawyer officers. Injustices would be minimized at the source, and investigating officers removed from command influence of unit commanders." [15] According to the American Civil Liberties Union, the institution of lawyer officers would not only "tend to assure the accused of compliance with his rights, but we feel it would eliminate much duplication of effort caused by unsound rulings at the investigation stage." [16]

Defining the court. It is critically important to insulate the system of military justice from command influence. This probably would require stripping the convening authority of his power to determine what type of court to convene; the present system enables him to indicate to court members his view of the gravity of the offense. Given two AWOL cases, one of which is sent to a special court and the other, seemingly similar in its facts, sent to a general court, the court members might well deduce the opinion of the convening authority. Not only does this give rise to the possibility of command influence, but it is an instance of "command justice" rather than military justice, since the punishments imposable by the two courts for the same offense are different. The present system gives the convening authority more than just the right to decide whether or not to prosecute a given case; it also gives him the choice as to where to prosecute. Georgetown law professor Joseph M. Snee, S.J., writes:

> The U.S. Attorney [in a civilian case] does not decide whether to send a case to district court or to the court of general sessions

on the grounds that he wants a greater or lesser punishment imposable. He looks at the punishment imposable under the statute
and that determines to which court it is sent.

Now when a commanding officer in two cases, which are similar
in nature, sends one to a summary court and the other to a general
court, the general court knows in advance the punishment that
the Commanding Officer thinks appropriate in that case. It is a
complete tipping of his hand, an indication by the fact that he
sent it to a general court rather than the special, that he thinks
the accused should get the maximum penalty.[17]

At least, it indicates that the convening authority concluded that
the defendant merited a sentence more severe than the six months'
confinement that is the maximum that a special court may impose.
As Professor Snee suggests, the determination of which court to be
employed should follow from the nature of the alleged crime and
the possible punishment.

CONVICTION WITHOUT TRIAL

The second major area of military justice that requires substantial change is the system of administrative discharges. These matters are (and according to General Hodson should be)[18] completely
outside the scope of the Uniform Code and thus do not afford the
accused who is to be "boarded" the rights that he would have if
his were a "criminal" offense. The accused may be given an undesirable discharge that may scar him for life, deprive him of GI
benefits, and leave him with no record upon which to base an
appeal. In the words of Senator Sam Ervin, of North Carolina:
"The undesirable discharge is under other than honorable conditions, is characterized by much of the same stigma as the dishonor-
able discharge, and, for purposes of veterans benefits and certain
other rights, is treated in the same way as a bad conduct discharge
imposed by a special court-martial."[19] Speaking as chairman of the
Subcommittee on Constitutional Rights, Senator Ervin pointed
out that the subcommittee has received "numerous complaints
that the safeguards of the Uniform Code have been circumvented
by the use of administrative discharge proceedings which are not
subject to these safeguards."[20] He concludes that "to the extent

that the armed services use administrative action to circumvent protections provided by the Uniform Code, the intent of Congress is thwarted and the constitutional rights of service personnel are jeopardized."[21]

Senator Tydings added that "we have a special responsibility to assure that those who risk their lives in defense of our democratic principles receive all of the blessings of these principles when called for in their own defense against criminal charges."[22]

Full protection of the Uniform Code should be extended to any serviceman facing a "boarding" that may result in a discharge under less than honorable conditions. Failing this, some intermediate steps would also improve the situation. First, the services should be required to give the affected serviceman in advance of the hearing a copy of the regulation or regulations under which he is to be "boarded." This is not always done under present procedures.[23] But how else can the man be expected to defend himself?

Further, since many of the servicemen involved in administrative proceedings are still in their teens, the parents or guardian should be notified before any serviceman who has not yet reached his majority can voluntarily accept a less than honorable discharge. In an address to a Congressional committee in 1966, Colonel D. George Paston, chairman of the Committee on Military Justice of the New York Lawyer's Association, stated: "From past experience, we have had too many cases of the boy gladly grabbing that opportunity, getting a discharge without honor and in later years coming to his Congressman and saying 'I can't get a job,' or 'I am barred from many other things because I was discharged without honor at the time.' At the time he was a boy and didn't realize its later importance."[24]

The American Legion goes a step further: "It is a contention of the American Legion that today, since the majority of persons in the military service are serving because they are drafted (or fear they will be) by draft boards of civilians in their own community, civilians should determine the type of discharge given from the military services if they receive a discharge other than an honorable discharge."[25]

"Boarding" procedures often deny servicemen the protections

of the Uniform Code, and Congress must act to redress this injustice.

EXTENDING THE BILL OF RIGHTS

Congress should also turn its attention to the censorship and repression of dissent within the military. In these areas the Code regulations are unduly restrictive and the services seem to be over-reaching.

News articles about the disciplining of antiwar newspaper editors and the censorship of service-network newscasts in Vietnam raise serious concern. Officials claim to censor military news on behalf of the morale of the men. But we may well ask if morale is not more seriously damaged when broadcasters reveal to the troops that the news has been censored. Even if full disclosure is not made, it is hardly likely that soldiers, always a perceptive and cynical bunch, will read sugarcoated news and not suspect it for what it really is.

Some of the tools for the repression of legitimate dissent come right out of the Uniform Code of Military Justice—and they should be removed. Article 88, "Contempt Toward Officials," states: "Any commissioned officer who uses contemptuous words against the President, the Vice-President, Congress, the Secretary of Defense, the Secretary of a military department, the Secretary of the Treasury, or the Governor or legislature of any State, Territory, or Commonwealth, or possession in which he is on duty or present shall be punished as a court-martial may direct." No wonder Professor Joseph W. Bishop, Jr., of Yale Law School, has "serious doubts" about its constitutionality.[26]

The basic problem with Article 88 is the vagueness of the offense. Article 133 is equally ambiguous; it authorizes the court-martialing of commissioned officers, cadets, and midshipmen for "conduct unbecoming an officer and a gentleman" without defining such conduct. And Article 134 is perhaps the most ill-defined of all:

> Though not specifically mentioned in this chapter, all disorders and neglects to the prejudices of good order and discipline in the armed forces, all conduct of a nature to bring discredit upon

the armed forces, and crimes and offenses not capital, of which persons subject to this chapter may be guilty, shall be taken cognizance of by a general, special, or summary court-martial, according to the nature and degree of the offense, and shall be punished at the discretion of that court.

To understand the implications of this article, compare it to a law passed in another nation thirty-five years ago:

If no definite penal law is immediately applicable to the [improper] act, the act shall be punished under the law which, according to the fundamental principles, applies to it most nearly.

That nation was Nazi Germany.

The special requirements of military life notwithstanding, it is high time for the Uniform Code of Military Justice to be brought more in line with the rights and freedoms of a democratic society.

ATTRACTING TOMORROW'S LEADERS

Not long ago at an Army base a young soldier said to a group of friends, "You know, before I came into the Army I was a conservative, but this place would make a radical out of anybody!"

Radical, conservative, apathetic—the consensus of the young men in the lower ranks of the service, whether draftee or enlistee, combat troop or typist, is that the system stinks. It is a verdict the military had better take into account for the day when it will have to depend totally on volunteers.

Nobody denies that a certain amount of griping has always gone on among the men in uniform; and certainly nobody expects the military to remake itself in the image of its PFCs. But the services must realize that the values of today's youth—honesty, equal opportunity, participation in the decisions that govern their lives—run head-on against the values of the NCOs they encounter in the military. It rests with these older men to make the services more appealing to young men; it is possible to keep in step with social change and still preserve the discipline and training necessary to the military.

Chapter 7

THE ENVIRONMENT

Give Earth a Chance

Not long ago in an eastern city a factory which lay idle during the daytime would belch smoke into the air after the sun went down. Apparently the plant's executives calculated that its rotten breath pouring into the air in the darkness of night would go undetected as a major cause of lung-destroying air. The ruse was uncovered by a resourceful group of young people who cranked a searchlight into action, illuminating the smokestacks in the middle of the night. Obviously the executives underestimated both the devotion of young people to the cause of a cleaner environment and their ingenuity in promoting it.

As the war in Vietnam began to fade as an issue among young people, many turned to ecological matters. After all, it is one issue on which people of all viewpoints can unite—we all have a stake in clean air and water, natural beauty, and an adequate food supply for the world. From Yippies to conservatives, young people have been flocking to the banner. To be sure, there are cynics who regard environmental issues as just another youthful fad, like the hula hoop or Tiny Tim. What these cynics fail to realize is that when young people embrace *political* issues—civil rights, peace, the environment—their commitment is total.

It is interesting to catalogue some of the activities of young people to popularize and promote this issue. The catalogue will be far from complete; some of the most important nationwide and regional efforts will not be noted, because our purpose here is to show how, in local areas and without prohibitive cost or effort, ingenuity can be translated into results.

Roots of Concern

What is it that attracts young people to the environment issue? For one thing, the young, with their great vitality, are more apt to love the outdoors, and have the time to enjoy it. The youth culture seeks to recapture the natural life: The great outdoors is the obvious alternative to an overly technological, overly bureaucratic society. Nature plays an important role in artistic works popular among the young, from Jack Kerouac's *On the Road* to the film *Easy Rider*. When asked why the young are interested in the environment, a girl replied, "We respect life. Green things. Being with nature. We like to be surrounded by green living things. We respect peace and peaceful things. Young people really enjoy life."

Second, young people are deeply worried about the long-term effects of pollution because they still have most of their lives ahead of them. The adult who drives a car, the mayor who fails to provide adequate sewage facilities, the manufacturer who defiles the air and water around his factory, may not worry about how they are ruining the world of fifty years hence. But young people worry. The destruction must stop. As President Nixon ominously noted, "It is literally now or never."

Young people echo this theme. In the words of a senior at Humboldt State College in northern California, "Five years ago when I became interested in the conservation movement I was primarily concerned with preserving wilderness and other areas that make life pleasant. Now I am primarily concerned with preserving life. If we are to maintain a livable environment on earth, we must radically change economic and social concepts in the United States and throughout the world. Token efforts will not do. We must launch a crash program for survival, including population stabilization and curtailment of the present rape of our natural environment. We are on a collision course with extinction. Either we change direction *now*, or we will go down."

Third, the fight for the environment is seen by many young people as another manifestation of their disagreement with older Americans' preoccupation with materialism. Beer cans littering our scenery, billboards defacing our parkways, inadequate social-welfare programs, ravenous factories, all epitomize the pursuit of wealth at the expense of social good. The ecological battle is in large part an educational effort to convince Americans that they must restrain their pursuit of the dollar if they are to have a livable world in which to enjoy their wealth.

A fourth motivation was expressed by a Stanford student: "The kids want to be involved in a relevant issue, one that matters. The students made an impact in Vietnam and now we want to show the establishment that they are wrong in their priorities. Only this time we are not talking about something thousands of miles away, like Vietnam, but right in their home towns."

And finally, after the deep national divisions of the 1960s, the young see the environment as one issue that can unite the nation— old and young, black and white, rich and poor, liberal and conservative. A student at Berkeley expressed it this way: "We can get the moderates to move with us for reform, not against us as it's been in the past. This is a national issue, one that can bring unity. Our rule of thumb is that you can trust the people."

THE RECORD OF LOCAL ACTIVISM

Every American produces one ton of solid waste per year. Hundreds of ancient redwoods topple because of the needless erosion of stream banks, in addition to the thousands that fall victim to the chain saw. The crab catch off San Francisco has dwindled dramatically, killed by insecticides sprayed on crops in the distant central valley of California. Soap suds piled up like snowbanks are found in streams and rivers throughout the country.

These and countless other environmental ills are now being paraded before the public, and no politician can afford to ignore them.

A classic example of a community spurred to action was the "Save Our Bay" fight in the San Francisco area in 1969. By the time the campaign to force the state legislature to act reached its peak, the entire state, comprising one of every ten Americans, was aware that the bay was in danger of being filled; only a narrow deepwater channel would remain.

Most of the San Francisco baylands are shallow marshlands.

Some areas have been filled in the past to build freeways, airports, industries, and even entire communities. In 1969 a crisis arose when the temporary agency that controlled the land-fill projects, the Bay Conservation and Development Commission, was scheduled to expire. The developers' lobby, especially influential in the state senate, was determined that the commission would not be preserved. Or, in case some legislation did squeak through, the lobbyists were confident that they could exert enough pressure to make the BCDC susceptible to all sorts of special interests.

A formidable campaign ensued to fight the developers. Not only is the bay a magnificent esthetic asset to its environs, but it contributes considerably to regulating the climate of the region. It is a major combatant of smog as well as an unequaled recreational resource. Its wildlife is abundant, with countless varieties of fish and fowl (and some of it is rare, including a red-bellied mouse which is the only land mammal on earth thriving on salt water).

When the Save Our Bay Action Committee was formed, within days thousands of young people wrote letters and telephoned the committee. They arrived at its headquarters to assist in the campaign to force the legislature to establish a permanent BCDC. Students from all over the state arrived to work in a desperate effort with radicals, liberals, moderates, and conservatives on the explosive fundamental issue of property rights. The efforts of these volunteers were supplemented when retired folk and parents became involved. They fanned out to ride commuter trains with pamphlets, bumper stickers, and petitions. Shopping centers in the Bay Area were deluged with literature. Thousands of pieces of mail were processed. Speeches were made before service clubs, schools, and church groups, and press releases were sent to newspapers. Not only were the key legislators, including the governor, swamped with visitors, but for every hearing held in Sacramento busloads of this great coalition converged on the capital. No politician having influence on the outcome was safe from public pressure.

The potency of the public sentiment became clear when the "Old Guard" legislators finally succumbed and enacted a law providing for a permanent agency to protect the bay.

Pacific Grove is a seaside community on the California coast north of the Big Sur country. The city council wanted to place a primary sewage outfall off the coast and hired a professional firm at a cost of $21,000 to advise on its placement. When the report was submitted, it was blasted by twelve students from the Stanford Hopkins Marine Laboratory, who had made their own study of water temperature and quality, currents and flow. They were able to prove to the council that if the outfall were constructed it would destroy the beach. They further showed the city a cheaper, long-range solution that included recycling for agricultural use. The facts presented by the students were unbeatable, and they prevailed.

Students in Cambridge, Massachusetts, organized the Boston Area Ecology Action, which last year picketed an international auto show to warn that "mixing auto exhaust and the air we breathe may be hazardous to your health." They also presented Boston Edison with a blue-ribbon pollution award for its contribution to the city's dirty air. Another Boston group called the Citizens for Participation in Politics mailed cards to Massachusetts residents on which violations of air-, water-, and noise-pollution laws and land-use regulations could be recorded and referred to the agency responsible. Neither group allowed the recent discovery of DDT in mothers' milk to pass unnoticed.

At the University of Minnesota concerned students buried the internal combustion engine in a mock funeral. Northwestern students organized in a drive to save Lake Michigan.

In 1970, San Fernando State College students commemorated the first anniversary of the Great Santa Barbara Oil Slick. One of the features was a giant balloon, representing the globe, covered with tar.

New Year's Eve, 1969, saw the culmination of nine two-day meetings held around the nation to select nine members for the Student Council on Pollution and the Environment (SCOPE), with the tenth appointed by Secretary of the Interior Hickel, to propose new schemes for a national clean-water campaign.

A beverage manufacturer found 26,000 cans on the lawn of his plant as University of Minnesota students protested the use of that indestructible packaging.

University of Texas students are publishing a state-wide environmental newsletter. The problems of preserving Puget Sound were spelled out in a report by University of Washington students.

Over $100,000 in foundation financing was raised by Cal Tech students by conducting an intercollegiate ecological research project. Two dozen groups have been organized at the University of Hawaii to deal with particular ecological problems.

A group in Berkeley, including students, convinced the city council to make a park on a barren two acres belonging to the Bay Area Rapid Transit District. Peoples Architecture, as they call themselves, wanted to set forth a positive expression on an issue very sensitive in that community—parks. Now the acreage will be green open space, not paved, as was the fate of People's Park. Another group is trying to set up a system with supermarkets and warehouses to save discarded cardboard and return it to the manufacturers for recycling. The same is being done with newspapers and aluminum cans. While their effort is considered token by some, they have been successful in making people conscious of each individual's one ton of refuse per year.

Another Berkeley student talked about the "food conspiracy" and his group's attempt to overcome it. Their objective is to purchase large quantities of food wholesale, grow some organically, bake bread, and operate the food bank as a co-op. The purpose would be to use fewer containers, provide more nutritious food, create less waste, and keep down the cost of eating.

A predictable offshoot of all this campus activity has been the press by students on school administrators and governing boards to provide courses in environmental sciences. At Berkeley a class on the natural resources ecosystem is the largest graduate course on campus, and related graduate and undergraduate courses are crammed full. San Francisco State has had a Department of Ecology and Systematic Biology for two years.

In November, 1969, the National Environmental Law Society was formed by ten law schools across the country to coordinate the efforts of local environmental law societies. The society aids attorneys bringing suit on environmental abuses and assists groups working for needed legislation. New courses are being demanded for their curriculums as well. A survey by Cornell University law students showed that one-third to one-half of 170 accredited law schools in the country will be giving courses in environmental law in the next academic year and that one-quarter of the 70,000 law students will enroll in these classes.

The University of Chicago Environmental Law Society documented criticism against the Federal Water Pollution Control Administration which, the society pointed out, had taken only one violator to court out of a possible forty-six cases. The society is preparing an environmental fact book listing all industries and municipalities in the Chicago area that are polluting lakes and streams. Another compilation lists banks and universities that hold major blocks of stock in offending companies.

Environmental law is new and poorly defined. A number of briefs are being prepared to test existing laws, set precedents, and explore the concept that the Constitution guarantees the right of all citizens to a decent and healthy environment.

To coordinate the data assembled by campus groups on specific targets, the Student Environmental Confederation was set up in November, 1969, with a membership of more than forty colleges and universities in California. The SEC will serve as a clearing house for information and projects, provide centralized public-relations and fund-raising services, operate a speakers' bureau, and maintain a valuable source of contact with government, nonprofessional organizations, and business. The intention of SEC is to create more public awareness of the environmental crisis through widespread education, lobbying, economic boycotts, and public demonstrations.

The SEC speaks as a unified voice representing the majority viewpoint—determined by referendum—of its members. At the time of its inception, the SEC set forth two general policy proposals:

> That due to the regional nature of most environmental problems which cut across older jurisdictional lines, regional government and thorough-going regional planning be immediately implemented as the most direct and appropriate institutional approach to the solution of these problems.
> That the state and the nation should reject the uncritical

objective of growth as it is deceptively measured in terms of GNP's and dollar standards of living, in favor of a policy which measures progress in terms of real increases in individual well-being, qualitative as well as quantitative.

In addition, specific legislative action has been proposed and is now the subject of intense lobbying, encompassing all the imaginative strategies of member groups of the SEC:

That a State Environmental Quality Agency be established which would bring an integrated, ecosystem approach to the environmental aspects of state policy decisions. Such an agency would be appointive, and its representation broad, both in terms of interests represented and professional expertise. This agency would be given a veto power over projects which did not conform with long-range state environmental interests.

That a tax be levied on products at the time of manufacture based on the cost of disposing of that product when it ultimately becomes solid waste. This would most easily be determined according to weight, figures such as a penny per pound being suggested as reflecting the actual cost of disposal.

That a tax should be levied on automobiles at the time of sale, based on the amount of effluents produced by that automobile. For autos using the internal combustion engine, this tax would be correspondingly quite high, thus creating a strong marketplace incentive for the development of low emission autos such as those powered by electricity, steam or gas turbines. This tax measure could be coupled with the eventual banning of internal combustion engines altogether as used in passenger cars.

That a tax should be levied on the sale of leaded gasoline to encourage the development of substitutes for the lead additive which has severe polluting effects.

That a deposit be required at the time automobiles are registered which would be returned only when the automobiles were properly disposed of, to curtail the practice of junking autos in the countryside.

That the state government establish a coastline commission along the lines of the Bay Conservation and Development Commission, which would have the power to determine matters of beach access, and development and use of the coastline.

That the government adopt a more positive approach to the subject of population control by legalizing all forms of birth control, including abortion, as a matter of basic human right. That the Federal and state tax structure be revised to discourage rather than encourage any increase in dependents. That the government pursue an active information campaign for the "prevention of unwanted children." That the provision in the California Health and Safety Code requiring all birth control devices to be sold only through pharmacists be eliminated.

Too Many People

It has been estimated that the earth can hold between six and eight billion people, but at enormous cost in terms of food supply and the preservation of a safe environment. Already experts are predicting that population growth will outstrip the food supply in India by 1975 and cause mass starvation.

Drawing their inspiration from the dramatic warnings of Stanford professor Paul Ehrlich, author of *The Population Bomb*, students are working to eliminate a root cause of our poisonous air and water, mountains of garbage, webs of concrete freeways, and inadequate housing—the population explosion. In a speech at San Francisco's historic Grace Cathedral, Mills College valedictorian Stephanie Mills, now working with Planned Parenthood of Alameda–San Francisco, noted that she could make no greater contribution to humanity than to refuse to bear children. During a conference at Stanford in the spring of 1969 attended by two hundred high-school and college students, the women in attendance made a pledge not to bear more than two children. And Dr. Lee A. Dubridge, then President Nixon's chief adviser on scientific matters, was the recipient of a "Where It's At" award given by a group calling itself Zero Population Growth. In accepting the award, Dr. Dubridge said, "Now for the first time in the earth's history there has emerged a creature for which fertility is not a blessing but a curse. That creature is man." The ZPG wants to reduce the birth rate to the point at which it equals the death rate.

This last point is crucial to an understanding of young people's attitudes toward population control and indeed all environmental issues. They have faced the monumental decisions and have made the hard choices. The decision to limit the size of one's family so that others may live is one such hard choice. In so doing, they reject the traditional American value that growth equals progress—whether growth in population, growth in technology, or growth in production. They will accept a lower standard of living rather than wear face masks and consume chemically created water and food.

At a November, 1969, meeting of the United States Commission for UNESCO in San Francisco, someone aptly pointed out that any population decline that is achieved would force a halt in the present direction of business growth. There were objections to industrial growth for its own sake, a prime target of young idealists. As one participant succinctly stated, "The very enunciation of this [suggestion]—the iconoclastic reiteration that there is another direction than mere arithmetical enlargement—appears to be the initial phase of the education process." A young Sierra Club member added, "We seek a planet on which the human population lives harmoniously, employing a sophisticated and unobtrusive technology which enhances rather than undermines the life-giving capability of the environment."

"Capitalism is predicated on money and growth, and when you're only interested in maximizing profits, you maximize pollution. We need a system that takes maximum care of the earth," said Cliff Humphrey, a leader of Ecology Action at Berkeley. Just as restraints were put on American industry to protect the investor during the New Deal, so will restraints have to be put on technology to protect all of us from a ravaged planet.

The young delegates at the UNESCO meeting formed a coalition and adopted a resolution listing the following demands:

A national policy to reverse America's population growth rate swiftly.

A massive federal study to determine the most sensible "carrying capacity" of the nation, based on quality of living for everyone, the tolerance of biological systems, and the impact of technology on world resources.

The abandonment of such concepts as gross national product and consumption of energy as indices of national growth.

A United Nations declaration that a "state of ecological emergency" exists on the planet.

A declaration by President Nixon to declare a state of environmental emergency.

A pledge to campaign for candidates whose views make "ecological sense."

A boycott of industries that pollute the environment.

The delegates called for teach-ins on college campuses and urban ghettos, for the formation of "ecological universities," and for the development of strong environmental programs at all levels of government. A young Sierra Club staffer said, "We have deep within us the ability to change ourselves and our culture. If man is to remain on earth he must transform his long urbanizing tradition into a new ecologically sensitive culture." An angry student from San Francisco State took a harder line: "We will stop the destruction of this planet even at the cost of our own futures, careers, and blood."

To Mobilize a Nation

Many Los Angeles playgrounds post the warning "Do not exercise strenuously or breathe too deeply during heavy smog conditions." It is conditions like this that cause so many young people to call for vast reform of the priorities set by the nation's leaders.

The well-publicized demonstrations by dissenting students have led many Americans to believe that these young people are radical bohemians urging wanton destruction of the American way of life. In light of this view, the impending ecological breakdown of the 1970s has given the idealistic young a unique opportunity—the opportunity to show their elders that they need to be saved from themselves, for in their relentless quest for material security they are raping the earth.

The young protesters insist that they want, not a new government, but one that respects them as human resources and protects their right to live full and productive lives in a life-giving and life-sustaining environment. They believe that we are in a life-and-death struggle to save nature and that no one should tolerate the blatant destruction of nature's bounty. They see such destruction as violence at its worst. This may be the crisis that unites mankind—already an incredible cross-section of the American people have joined forces to combat this problem.

And so, regardless of whether Ralph Nader continues to lead protest marches in front of General Motors or regardless of whether the youth of the nation flock to candidates sympathetic to the earth, changes of vast proportions are bound to occur in the 1970s because of the power attained by youth in the last decade. President Nixon acknowledged this when he referred to the "protest ethic" existing among the young; he noted that this can help the nation so long as it is channeled within the system. This advice is particularly appropriate to environmental reform; the chaos that pervades this field must be transmuted into an orderly process.

Politicians must take heed of this, for the young have already shown their political potency. The President too is vulnerable, for several of his potential rivals in the next election distinguished themselves on the environmental issue long before the burst of publicity began in 1969. Young people are noted for their skepticism toward established leaders; any politician who would garner votes on this issue must demonstrate a sincere commitment to reclaiming the earth. Some of the most exciting of the younger Republican officeholders—Representative Pete McCloskey, of California, and Governor Francis Sargent, of Massachusetts, to name two—come equipped with expertise on ecology.

Scientists at the 1969 Governor's Conference on California's Changing Environment stated that unless environmental reform is undertaken immediately, in ten years the nation will be at the point of no return. Government at all levels may be facing its most severe test with this issue, as younger citizens evaluate its credibility and its ability to respond. But the Save the Bay issue in San Francisco went a long way to prove the efficacy of "working within the system": Dramatic results *can* occur within the democratic process.

Many citizens "over thirty" have learned effective techniques from the young activists: Sit-ins, street demonstrations, petitions, and the like were used by prominent citizens in Santa Barbara in Project GOO—Get Oil Out—when their beaches were ruined by an oil spill early in 1969. In the Corte Madera creekbed in a California suburb near San Francisco, social, business, and political leaders sat in front of earth movers to protest an Army Corps of Engineers flood-control project that failed to take into account the ensuing effects on the ecology of the area.

Will the nation's business community in partnership with the government provide the necessary solutions to heal the dying earth? In short, will the year 1980 see an America that has decided to be worthy of the magnanimous grant of land we inhabit?

Chapter 8

YOUTH IN POLITICS

The Politics of Commitment

"The trouble with you young people," said a sympathetic Congressman to a group of activists in his office last year, "is that you take what older people say too seriously."

This wry comment has a great deal of truth in it:

In the 1950s social commentators complained that young people constituted a "silent generation" and lacked interest in the serious issues of the day; today young people are more involved in politics than any previous generation in history. Politicians, teachers, parents, all claimed that America is a nation that believes in peace and racial equality; so young activists went out and stirred up the entire country trying to make reality conform to these beliefs. Civics textbooks stated that American government is based on popular rule and citizen participation; so youth organized a campaign that ultimately forced a President to retire.

And now older Americans criticize these young people for being *too* active, for taking what they were taught seriously.

Why have young people, in one brief decade, become so involved in the great political issues of the day? How has their involvement in those issues changed over the years? Are they a threat to traditional patriotic values and the stability of the political system, or are they an affirmation that the American system can accommodate the demands of all the people?

THE REWARDS OF INVOLVEMENT

It should be made clear at the outset that this is *not* a study of the political attitudes of the mass of American youth. Rather, it focuses on the minority of young people who have become political "activists," who have already made an indelible mark on American political history.

Furthermore, we are not primarily concerned with young people who become part of the traditional political system, as young people have always done. Every major campaign has its young volunteers who lick envelopes and hang posters; every candidate has his bright young aides. But these are young people who have chosen to become auxiliaries in an operation run by adults, and their contribution is not basically different from the work of older envelope-lickers and staff assistants.

Instead, we shall discuss genuine political *youth* movements— movements led by young people, staffed by young people, and involved in issues that appeal especially to young people.

Young people have been involved in political campaigns before, notably those of Wendell Willkie and Adlai Stevenson. But in 1968 came a genuine departure—the Presidential campaign of Eugene McCarthy, which was not only manned by young people but planned and managed by them as well. And the dominant issue—peace—was a "youth" issue.

But to focus on candidates and personalities is to miss a fundamental point—that young people in the last ten years have become involved in politics out of a concern with issues, not personalities. In 1968 it was not charismatic Robert Kennedy, but soft-spoken peace candidate Eugene McCarthy who gained the loyalty of the best of the young activists. One of the most revealing moments in Kennedy's campaign was his encounter with a couple of fervent teenaged McCarthy volunteers in Indiana; he could not understand why they preferred McCarthy, when so many voters were attracted to the Kennedy cause. The reason, they explained, was that McCarthy had been "first" on the peace issue.

Who are these new activists? They are mainly students and graduates of our colleges and universities. Indeed, a Gallup poll reported in May, 1969, that more than one-fourth of College students had participated in a demonstration of some kind during their college careers.[1]

The activists are a minority among young people, but do they speak only for themselves? Or do they represent a wide spectrum of the views of their peers? The Louis Harris poll provided a partial answer in November, 1969, when it asked Americans whether they sympathized with antiwar demonstrators. While the nation as a whole divided evenly between sympathy and disagreement, twenty-to-thirty-year-olds supported the activists, 59 to 34 percent.[2]

If we are to understand the motives of these young activists, we might list three basic reasons why people in general involve themselves in political activity:

The short-run aim. Most older people in politics have limited objectives in mind—public office, passage of a particular bill or policy, a patronage job, and so on. Their motivation need not be selfish: They may seek office out of a desire for public service or hope to implement a particular policy because it will fulfill the public interest.

The long-run aim. Sometimes a politician will advocate a position not because it is likely to have immediate effect, but because he feels that he is helping to bring about a change some time in the future. Young people are more likely than their elders to get involved in this kind of issue. For one thing, the idea of selfless advocacy of long-range reform appeals to the idealism of young people. Moreover, the young adult is likely to live to see the results of long-run changes. And so he becomes interested in issues that affect the distant future—conservation and pollution, population control, nuclear fallout, urban planning, the quality of American life. "In the long run," said Lord Keynes, "we are all dead." But young people expect to live to see that long run.

Self-expression. This is a type of political activity almost exclusively indulged in by the young. It is a product of the fervent desire of young people to inject honesty into politics; they have seen enough hypocrisy. It often means making a statement or gesture that may antagonize potential supporters, but it is justified on the grounds that it is an honest act. For example, a young person discussing the war in Vietnam believes that the United States is improperly interfering in a civil war among Vietnamese. But in his desire to express his views with fearless honesty he does not make the point in such guarded language. Instead he may say,

"The United States is an imperialist power exploiting the people of Vietnam." The language is more blunt and, some would say, exaggerated, but its very tone makes the young person feel that he is being true to his innermost convictions.

The fear of compromising honesty is the crux of the matter. Because the "art" of compromise has led to so many disappointments and sellouts in traditional politics, young people are sometimes determined to avoid anything that remotely resembles compromise, even at the risk of offending those whom they hope to persuade. And the politics of self-expression is the result.

Of course, the politics of self-expression includes, on the outer fringes, activities that are bizarre and sometimes violent or illegal —from shouting down a speaker, to burning draft cards, to calls for armed insurrection. Such acts are the result of the frustration felt by young people who have become disillusioned with a political system that is unresponsive to the need for change.

One basic danger is that the mass media have a propensity to focus on such acts rather than on the more subdued activity of most activists. Often the fact that a Viet Cong flag appeared in a peace parade pre-empts the more significant news that the overwhelming majority of paraders opposed such an inflammatory action.

What is critical to remember, then, is that activists are predominantly *not* extremists, *not* in favor of violence, and *not* anti-American. It has been remarked that the highest form of patriotism is the desire to reform the nation so that it will live up to its highest principles. This is the idea expressed in the youth slogan, "America—change it or lose it."

Early Years: Commitment to Equal Rights

Before the 1960s young people were involved in politics only infrequently and in subordinate ways. Campaigns like those of Willkie and Stevenson and organizations like the National Committee for a Sane Nuclear Policy and Turn Toward Peace were run by older people; and party offshoots, from the Young Republicans to the Young Communist League, had little or no power of their own.

Toward the end of the "silent" 1950s a generation that had grown up in the prosperity of the postwar era reached college age. These young people differed from previous generations in their formative experiences, not having known the economic problems of a depression, the devastation of a world war, or the fear of political witch-hunting in the early 1950s. Furthermore, they grew up at a time when the struggle for racial equality—the *Brown v. Board* decision, Little Rock, the Montgomery bus boycott—was capturing headlines and provoking discussion throughout the nation.

All these factors produced a large group of college students who were idealistic, ready to join a cause, and inspired by the courageous efforts of black people in the South to share in the American dream. All that was needed was a spark.

That spark came at the beginning of the new decade, in the first months of 1960, in Greensboro, North Carolina. Four black freshmen from a nearby college sat down at a segregated Woolworth's lunch counter and remained even after the management refused to serve them. They continued their protest, despite attacks by white hoodlums and a bomb threat, until the police closed the store.

The tactic spread—to other students in Greensboro, to the rest of North Carolina, to neighboring states, finally throughout the South. Almost immediately white students, North and South, joined sit-ins and picket lines. At first the Northerners protested in their own cities. Then a few began to go South to where the action was, and a new breed—the freedom rider—was born.

At this point, it is important to recall the tone and orientation of the fledgling civil-rights movement. Jack Newfield described it in this way: "The early sit-in activist was surprisingly middle class and patriotic. He was always well groomed and wore a suit and tie when demonstrating. Often he read the Bible or a copy of the Constitution while sitting at the lunch counter. If he broke his disciplined decorum to sing at the moment of arrest, it was often a patriotic anthem."[3] Newfield also stresses that the sit-in movement "never became overtly political."[4] Instead, it was a spontaneous movement that grew out of the moral concerns of young blacks and whites and whose principal tactic was, if anything, economic.

The most telling point of all, in light of subsequent developments, was that the early civil-rights movement was "as American as cherry pie." It was nonviolent and biracial. Furthermore, it was aimed at arousing the sympathy of all Americans, since the American people, the President, Congress, the Supreme Court, and both political parties said they favored racial equality.

But it is also important to note how uniquely youthful was the nature of the movement:

From the start, the Southern black youth rallied to a new civil-rights organization, the Student Nonviolent Coordinating Committee (SNCC), founded in October, 1960, in Atlanta.

The aims of the sit-in movement—the dramatization of racial injustice, the mobilization of public sympathy—were typically "youthful" political aims, self-expression and long-range reform.

The movement caused a rift between the black activists and their cautious parents, who were accused of being too concerned with material comfort and not concerned enough with human rights (even their own). As Martin Luther King, Jr., said in 1960, "The sit-in movement is a revolt against those Negroes in the middle class who have indulged themselves in big cars, and ranch-style homes, rather than joining in the movement for freedom."[5]

This is not the place to document the many events and acts of courage that distinguished the civil-rights movement of the early 1960s. Suffice it to say that it was the beginning of the political activation of American youth, black and white. In the early years, however, four trends developed:

The violence directed against civil-rights workers led to increased frustration and militancy. In parts of the South blacks organized armed defense against the night riders.

Many in the movement began to see poverty, and not only racism, as the key to the problem. And so civil-rights volunteers began to work in the rural areas of the South, where poverty was most severe.

Electoral politics was another recourse, and SNCC and other groups concentrated on voter-registration drives (at great danger to life and property). In Mississippi blacks and their white supporters founded the Mississippi Freedom Democratic party (MFDP) to run candidates against the establishment Democrats in primaries. And so Julian Bond and Charles Evers were elected to public office in the South.

And finally, it was the MFDP that led to the most far-reaching development in the movement—disillusionment with American liberalism. In 1964 the civil-rights movement was cruelly disappointed when the MFDP sought seats at the 1964 Democratic convention, to replace the party of James Eastland: A "compromise" engineered by the old champion of civil rights, Hubert H. Humphrey, gave the MFDP only "symbolic" representation in the lily-white delegation. As Stokely Carmichael and Charles V. Hamilton later wrote: "But the MFDP did not go to the Convention as a symbolic act; it went in a sincere effort to become part of the national Democratic party. . . . If anything was a symbolic act, it was the stand taken by the national party: a stand which clearly said 'betrayal' and clearly symbolized the bankruptcy of the Establishment." [6] This event was the clearest symptom of the growing estrangement between black aspirations and white liberalism, and presaged the call by Carmichael and others for black separatism.

For white student activists the year 1963 marked a crucial turning point in their political development. In that year three events occurred that laid the seeds for a momentous transition: The activists would no longer be content to work through established institutions to bring about change; they now espoused a more radical approach that would bring them in conflict with both the government and society.

One of those events was, of course, the murder of the President. John F. Kennedy had forged a strong link between young people of widely varying backgrounds and their government. His blend of liberalism and virility had something for almost all young people. His death deprived America's youth of this living proof of the good faith of the nation's leaders. His successor seemed to be a throwback to the days when government was run by old men insensitive to the needs of young people. And this had profound implications for the future of youthful activism for, as one peace leader put it, had it been John Kennedy rather than Lyndon

Johnson who escalated the war in Vietnam after the Tonkin Gulf incident, it would have been far more difficult to recruit young people to oppose the war.

The second event of 1963, the civil-rights march on Washington in August, is seen in retrospect as the apex of the civil-rights movement. The march climaxed the nonviolent and biracial phase of black America's struggle for equality. Afterward came the northern ghetto riots, black militancy, and the black separatist organizations.

The march had two long-range effects on the political activity of youth: It set a precedent for future demonstrations, notably the Poor People's March of 1968 and the November, 1969, peace moratorium; and it marked the end of white participation in the civil-rights movement.

The second effect was a by-product of the growing militancy of young blacks. White liberals were informed that the days of biracialism in the civil-rights movement were over; that blacks had to secure their rights on their own. In 1966 Stokely Carmichael was chosen chairman of SNCC; his election transformed SNCC into a black-power organ. And so the white veterans of freedom rides and sit-ins either took to organizing poor whites or turned to the peace movement.

The third event of 1963 was the signing of the nuclear test-ban treaty. Peace activists had participated in Ban the Bomb movements such as the Committee for a Sane Nuclear Policy. With the ratification of the ban on nuclear testing, they, like their white civil-rights colleagues, were more or less set adrift in search of a new cause.

And that cause arose in the years after 1963 and grew until it galvanized American youth as no political issue had ever done: The new President, Lyndon Johnson, turned to a smoldering war in Southeast Asia and made it his own—with enormous consequences for his own political career and for the political development of America's youth.

OPPOSITION TO THE WAR

It is difficult to discuss the history of the movement against the

Vietnam war. A task-force report to the National Commission on the Causes and Prevention of Violence noted: "Indeed, the movement is best understood as a result of events, not as a generator of future actions ... There is little general agreement about the makeup and nature of the Vietnam protest movement ... The more one learns about the organizational structure and development of the peace movement, the more reluctant one must be to speak of its concerted direction."[7]

Throughout the 1960s, three trends were on the rise: America's involvement in the Vietnam war; the number and size of demonstrations to protest this development; and the opposition of the American people at large to the war.

It is important to note how the peace movement compared with the earlier civil-rights movement. To be sure, the peace movement was by and large motivated by the same idealistic concerns that had characterized the rights movement. American support of undemocratic regimes in Saigon, the killing of civilians, the burning of villages, the use of napalm, and the inability of the Johnson administration to justify convincingly our role in the war—all these factors aroused the righteous indignation of hundreds of thousands of young Americans. But a critical difference from the earlier movement was that whereas the struggle for civil rights was waged under the aegis of a sympathetic federal government and a tolerant public, the peace movement brought young Americans into conflict with their government and most of their elders. This simple fact is perhaps the key to the nature of the movement. It explains, for one thing, why the peace movement so often devolved into the politics of self-expression, the desperate gestures of young men and women whose government had, in the name of peace, embarked upon a futile, wasteful, self-destructive war.

Surely there have been unpopular wars in our history—the nineteenth century had four of them. But the world wars of our own century were marked by fervent patriotism, and many older Americans are accustomed to thinking of wars as necessary evils which all citizens have a duty to support. Young Americans, however, have no memory of "necessary" wars; they believe the individual should obey the dictates of his conscience.

There was another important difference between the two movements: Unlike the civil-rights workers, the peace activists could
anticipate little likelihood of incremental change. In the civil-rights
movement, the integration of a public facility or the enrollment
of a few black voters marked real progress. Even though such
advances did not in themselves revolutionize Southern race relations, the civil-rights workers could feel that some progress had
been accomplished, and could summon the will to continue working within the system. But the peace movement had no such
victories. As long as the war continued, there was no progress at all.
This lack of accomplishment certainly fed the flames of the politics
of frustration.

The purpose of the peace movement was, until 1968, to rally
American public opinion against the administration. Peace marches
were to demonstrate strength in numbers; teach-ins were to edu-
cate. But it was not until the Tet offensive of February, 1968, that
the mass of Americans began to turn decisively against the war.

In that year, the leaders of the peace movement, like Southern
blacks before them, turned to the electoral process for redress.
While a revolution in Southern politics requires a vast multitude
of state and local electoral victories, de-escalation of the war required a change in only one office—the Presidency of the United
States.

It was at that time, in the winter of 1967–68, that the strategy
of the activists coincided with the ambitions of Senator Eugene
McCarthy, of Minnesota, who sought to deprive the President of
his party's nomination.

CLIMAX AND DENOUEMENT

The McCarthy movement was a last-ditch attempt by the peace
movement to work within the respectable, systemic norms in which
the civil-rights movement had operated. For one thing, campaign-
ing for a Presidential candidate was an indication that young
people had not given up on the American political system. And
the personal grooming that the McCarthy leaders required of
canvassers ("Be Clean for Gene") indicated a desire to put pragmatism over self-expression for the time being.

The results were historic. In one near-victory the youthful McCarthy canvassers electrified the nation and sent Lyndon Johnson on his swift road to retirement (and de-escalation of the war). Other candidates, notably Robert Kennedy and Nelson Rockefeller, began to woo the peace vote. Each of them picked up large numbers of youthful adherents. But it was McCarthy who, by his quixotic entry into the race before anyone suspected the size of the peace vote, secured the allegiance of most of the activists. Small wonder that in a poll taken in October, 1968, McCarthy was admired by more college students than any other major politician.[8]

As the preconvention campaign wore on, disillusionment began to set in. For one thing, Robert Kennedy, seen by the McCarthy people as an opportunistic Bobby-come-lately, began to defeat McCarthy in primaries. And even more distressing was the number of convention votes amassed by Hubert Humphrey, who had never entered a primary. The McCarthy people were learning, the hard way, the oligarchic nature of Presidential nominating politics.

But it was not until the Chicago convention that the final profound disillusionment came. For it was then that the conflict between young activists and the government reached a bloody climax.

Even today, several years after the event, those clashes between police and demonstrators arouse controversy. Surely there were cases of extreme provocation by demonstrators. But most impartial observers, including the Walker Commission and the news media, concur that the Chicago police indulged in unnecessary and usually unprovoked brutality. A host of leading Democrats, including governors, senators, and mayors, criticized the police in strong language. Even Ronald Reagan, perennial supporter of everyone's local police, conceded that "there were probably some individual policemen who overly reacted."[9]

These events, combined with the boss tactics used to nominate Humphrey, proved to be the climax of the growing alienation of activists from mainstream politics. The brutality of the police, condoned by the Presidential nominees, served notice that young protesters would no longer be welcome in the land of the free.

It is impossible to overstress the change in attitude of many activists—their worst suspicions about the American "power elite" were confirmed in the streets of Chicago. As one twenty-six-year-old witness said: "This convinced me that the system couldn't be changed, that the police state that existed outside the convention also extended inside, that we would have to defend ourselves or be wiped out."[10] Perhaps most activists did not share her despair, but certainly the precedent for official violence has been set, and will forever threaten future demonstrations. This is a source of increasing despair among young liberals.

What is in store for the activists?

There will be no lack of causes to embrace. Peace protests will continue as long as the war does, although with diminishing strength. Electoral politicking will continue. Other concerns, notably environmental ones, will replace the war as the primary political issue.

But one thing is certain: The fire that was ignited by the spark in Greensboro, North Carolina, in 1960 will rage for a long time to come.

THUNDER LEFT AND RIGHT

The foregoing account of student activism concentrated on the largest group, the slightly left-of-center liberals who have generally worked within the American reform tradition, but with a new style and level of commitment. The reader may well wonder, What about the far left and the far right? Are they merely the latest version of older movements, or do they share typically "youthful" traits with their liberal contemporaries?

The New Left. In discussing the youthful far left, we shall concentrate on the group that has attracted the most attention of all, Students for a Democratic Society (SDS). It is not essential to the discussion to recount the history, ideology, and factions of SDS; perhaps the best way to generalize about it would be to concentrate on what distinguishes it from older radical movements.

Whereas the old left was dogmatic, highly theoretical, and well versed in Marxist lore, SDS has been since its inception in the early 1960s a loose coalition of individuals who eschew dogma and search for highly personal ways to revolutionize society. It is, above all, the politics of self-expression, and reading Marx and Trotsky is not an exercise in self-expression.

The SDS insistence on free self-expression has led to: a firm belief in participatory democracy and maximum control by the individual of his life, the lack of a hard-and-fast political program and the refusal of SDS to require its members to adhere to any line, and the search for new life-styles and types of social organization, such as communes and new organizations of the poor.

Such organizational looseness has led to intense factionalism, which culminated in the splintering of SDS in 1969. It has also been partly responsible for three charges that have been leveled at SDS: that they offer no "constructive program," only negative criticisms of American society; that they favor violent methods to achieve their goals; and that they are Communists, or tools of Communist infiltrators.

The first criticism, that SDS has no concrete program for a better society, is often made by older radicals who feel that SDS lacks ideological discipline. Yet a movement that is devoted to individual self-expression would hamstring itself if it formulated a blueprint that may be unsuited to every individual and to unforeseen events. It has been one of the strengths of the New Left that it has promised only to release the capabilities of every individual and has not tried to dictate what the individual will do with his capabilities.

As for violence, it is an unfortunate byproduct of the ideological looseness of SDS that certain factions, notably the notorious Weathermen, hold that only violent revolution can lead to constructive social change. Most adherents of SDS do *not* advocate violence, except in self-defense; but the public image of SDS is fostered by visions of Weathermen running wildly through city streets, smashing windows, bombing buildings, fighting police.

Both the police and those who would summon them at the slightest sign of trouble must realize that every time official force is misused (at the Chicago convention, at Berkeley's People's Park), new violence-prone radicals are created. Wayne Morse has commented that American foreign policy has created more Communists abroad than Soviet foreign policy has; similarly, the Chicago police have created more militants than the Weathermen could ever have recruited.

Finally, SDS is accused of being Communist-dominated, that

old familiar smear. It should be evident that in their lack of discipline and refusal to be bound by Marxist gospel the young radicals of SDS would be misfits in the rigid Communist party structure. Furthermore, SDS passes the acid test of non-Communism by criticizing the Soviet Union for violating basic freedoms. In its natal declaration, the Port Huron Statement, SDS declared its opposition to the USSR because of its "total suppression of organized opposition," and SDS has been vocal in criticizing the Soviet bureaucracy and the invasion of Czechoslovakia in 1968. They regard the Communist party of the United States as a bunch of tired, unimaginative old men.

SDS has refused to raise barriers against Communists joining their movement because they are unwilling to close their doors to any converts. And they regard the fear of "contamination" by Communism felt by older left-liberals as an irrelevant hangover from the days of Joe McCarthy.

The New Right. Just as the older left has given way to a unique youth movement, so the young conservatives have their own organization, Young Americans for Freedom (YAF). Conservatism is traditionally associated with older people, and the notion of a youth movement of the right may strike some people as paradoxical. Furthermore, conservatives, precisely because they oppose liberal and radical proposals for change, are often rather subdued and do not engage in activism.

What attracts young people to conservatism? Perhaps the answer is summed up by a well-known right-wing activist, Lee Edwards: "There's so much happening, changing. It's not so much a matter of conserving, but of extending freedom. Today a conservative has to be a radical." [11]

Surely the notion of the conservative as radical hints at why young people are attracted to the creed. For if political-minded youth seek to reform the system, and that system is New Deal liberal, then one avenue of change is from the right.

Moreover, YAF employs many of the tactics of the liberal activists: Civil-rights advocates boycotted segregated businesses; YAF members boycott firms dealing with Communist countries. Peace advocates demonstrate against the war; YAF members march in support of hawkish policies. And even the McCarthy "children's campaign" was predated by a large youth involvement in the Gold-water campaign (although that campaign, unlike the McCarthy campaign, was planned by older people).

But to understand fully why young people are attracted to YAF, we must understand a basic split in American conservatism. This philosophy has two roots: older European conservatism, which emphasized tradition, a rigid class structure, and a disdain for commercialism; and American laissez-faire capitalism, which claims a libertarian heritage descended from John Stuart Mill and Adam Smith.

It is the existence of these two strains that has led to splits within YAF as bitter as those within SDS. Some members of YAF, deeply committed to the libertarian strain of conservatism, have broken away and formed the Student Libertarian Alliance (SLA). Anti-government to the core, they oppose higher taxes, punitive drug laws, harassment of hippies, and the military-industrial complex.

Small surprise, then, that young people are being drawn to libertarian conservatism, for they share the desire for individual freedom and self-expression that motivates the New Left. This common bond is exemplified by Karl Hess, a former Goldwater aide who is now a New Leftist, and who has invited Senator Gold-water to join the New Left because of that common bond. Small wonder, also, that just as older leftists denounce SDS for its lack of ideology and discipline, the older conservatives of *National Review* denounce the SLA as "anarchists, more or less," and called their program "ideological totalism ... an ideological trip." [12]

ACTIVISTS AND THE FUTURE OF AMERICAN POLITICS

Let us conclude with a note about the effect of all this on the future of American politics. There are several trends that hint at changes to come:

Young people are more and more loath to identify with a political party. A recent Gallup poll found a majority of college students refusing to call themselves Republicans or Democrats,[13] and a study of the 1968 elections by the Survey Research Center noted that voters in their twenties were least likely of all age groups to possess party identification.[14]

Underlying this voting independence is a lack of faith in our political institutions. Another Gallup poll of college students found that only 18 percent had a favorable reaction to political parties (this was not a radical group; 56 percent were favorable to business).[15]

Furthermore, students are becoming more and more polarized in their political beliefs. In 1966 an American Council on Education survey of college freshmen found that 65 percent described themselves as "middle of the road"; in 1969 that figure dropped to 44 percent (most of the movement was to the left).[16]

Such disaffection with the political system does not merely affect today's politics. Today's youthful demonstrators are tomorrow's national leaders:

Already men have been elected to Congress who first voted in 1960, the year in which John F. Kennedy was elected President.

Within ten years we will have our first Congressmen who were born after World War II, and who came of age during the Vietnam war and a period of intense racial strife.

Within fifteen years we are likely to have a President who grew to manhood at the time of the Kennedy assassination, the escalation of the war in Vietnam, and the birth of the black-power movement. His perspective on the world will be framed by those events, just as today's leaders think in terms of parallels with the Great Depression and World War II.

In short, the time is near when the committed generation will be old enough to exert general political power through the electoral process. How the government and the rest of society reacts to them today will determine American politics for decades to come.

Chapter 9

LEGAL RIGHTS

Eighteen as the Age of Maturity

*This chapter was prepared before the United States Supreme Court upheld the right of 18-year-olds to vote in national elections. We retain it because the arguments are equally valid for state and local elections.—*ED.

For the young people of Great Britain, New Year's Day, 1970, was the dawning of an age of new rights and responsibilities. On that day, the age of legal maturity was lowered from 21 to 18.

As *The New York Times* correspondent wrote, "Three million young people are eligible to vote, hold and dispose of property, make binding contracts, make wills, marry without the consent of parents or court, donate blood and make purchases on the installment plan. They may also be sent circulars from bookmakers and be hypnotized for the purpose of public entertainment. And for the first time, they can be sued if they default on their debts." [1]

If Britain, with its socially conservative traditions, can change its laws in such a liberal, youth-oriented direction, the United States can surely follow suit. In this chapter, we present the case for granting the franchise and other paramount legal rights to 18-year-olds.

ROOTS OF A TRADITION

It is revealing to note how the age of 21 came to be accepted as the age of majority in America, and indeed, in most of the Western world. Since the age of 21 was adopted in colonial times, it would seem to derive from Anglo-Saxon tradition, and here a British Parliamentary "Report of the Committee on the Age of Majority" [2] is illuminating:

> Roman historians state that the barbarians reckoned their young were old enough to carry arms and be counted as grown up at 15. And 15 became the general age of majority in Britian and Northern Europe during the 9th, 10th and 11th centuries, though not specifically linked with fighting ability. But by the time of the Norman Conquest there was a change of emphasis. The role of the mounted knight became more and more important, and armour heavier and heavier, and the horses more enormous as time went on. By the time of Magna Carta the age for those holding in knight service had been raised to 21, and there is strong authority for the view that this was directly linked with the ability to hold up a heavy suit of armour and lift a lance or sword at the same time.

For the common people, who could not aspire to knighthood, the age of maturity remained at 15. So it is evident that 21 as the age of legal maturity is a vestige of the feudal age having little relevance to our own day. However, tradition is a heavy weight to bear, and the case for change must be well justified if it is to be overcome.

THE VOTE

The history of America has been marked by a gradual expansion of the right to vote and the removal of barriers against it. The next step in this process may well be the removal of the age barrier.

There is great support for such a change. Since 1939 the Gallup Poll has surveyed public opinion on the 18-year-old vote. In 1939 only 17 percent of respondents approved; by 1967 it was up to 64 percent. Georgia and Kentucky now have the 18-year-old vote; Hawaiians may vote at 20 and Alaskans at 19. Recent referenda in Hawaii, North Dakota, Nebraska, and Ohio only narrowly defeated a bill for the 18-year-old vote. In 1970 voters in Alaska, Connecticut, Hawaii, Maine, Massachusetts, Minnesota, Montana, Nebraska, Oregon, South Dakota, Washington, and Wyoming decided the issue.

Among the advocates of the 18-year-old vote have been Presidents Eisenhower, Johnson, and Nixon, and Presidential aspirants Goldwater, Rockefeller, Romney, and Humphrey. In the Ninety-first Congress, sixty-six Senators and seventy-eight Representatives from all parties, regions, and ideologies sponsored Constitutional amendments aimed at lowering the voting age nationwide. More than two-thirds of the state governors support a younger vote in their states.

What are the arguments for lowering the voting age to 18? Perhaps the most frequently stated is one that President Eisenhower gave in his 1952 campaign: "If young men 18 or 19 are old enough to . . . fight their country's battles . . . then they are old enough to take part in the political life of their country and to be full citizens with voting powers." [3]

But when advocates of the 18-year-old vote use this emotional argument, they leave themselves open to legitimate criticism. Representative Emanuel Celler, chairman of the House Judiciary Committee, cogently argued in a radio debate: "To say that he who is old enough to fight is old enough to vote is to draw an utterly fallacious parallel. No such parallel exists. The ability to choose, to separate promise from performance, to evaluate on the basis of facts, are the prerequisites to good voting age . . . The thing called for in a soldier is uncritical obedience, and that is not what you want in a voter." [4]

The more valid defense of the 18-year-old vote is the argument that today young people possess at 18 the level of education, information, and awareness of public issues that their parents had at 21. For example, more than three out of four people in the age group 18 to 20 are high school graduates; almost half are in college. The median school years completed is 12.2 years. In 1962 a survey revealed that 80 percent of young people read ten or more books a year, 78 percent read a newspaper every day, and 73 percent read at least one magazine regularly. [5]

The outcome in one state that has allowed its 18-year-old to vote is illuminating. "It has been my experience in Kentucky," former Senator Thruston B. Morton said, "that the dropouts, the kids that are sent to reform school and the general deadbeats don't register and don't participate in political activities. The high

school graduates, especially those that go on to college, do take
advantage of the voting privilege . . . From a standpoint of intelligence and educational background, they are probably better
qualified to pass judgment on issues and to assess personalities than
the average voter in the state."

In 1969 a group of young Republican Congressmen toured over
fifty colleges and reported their findings to the President: "There
is no question that the American college student for the most part
is better educated and more vitally concerned with contemporary
problems in our country than at any previous time in our history.
We feel that active involvement in the political process can constructively focus his idealism on the most effective means of change
in a free society." [6]

Some of the arguments used against the vote are particularly
smug and insulting. Foremost in this category is the argument that
18-year-olds might not use the franchise "responsibly." By this
token, one might question how many adults can be called "responsible," especially those who never vote (one out of three eligible
voters!) or those who never participate in any political activity
except to vote as knee-jerk partisans year after year. The common
estimate among politicians is that one out of four voters falls into
this category, and that straight party voting is most typical of older
voters. This means that about half of America's adults do not exercise the minimum activity of responsible citizenship—a thoughtful, considered vote.

Throughout American history the charge of irresponsibility has
been leveled at groups which sought entry into the political
process. First it was the propertyless, then former slaves, then
women. History confirms that the kind of political leadership produced by their votes was not worse—and often it was better—than
the leadership elected before they were enfranchised. For many
people, mere exposure to the responsibility of the ballot inspires
intelligent participation.

Another argument against the 18-year-old vote is that the voting
booth is too important to be used as a training ground for citizenship. Dr. Kenneth Colegrove of Northwestern University offered
a typical analogy in 1954: "If the argument [for participation] is
valid, young men would be put into the first line of the football

team right at the very beginning, instead of being given a long training and practice beforehand. Football and voting are very different matters, but the more schooling a man has—the more experience a person has—before he exercises this privilege, rather than a right of voting, the better he will perform." [7]

What Dr. Colegrove seems to be suggesting is an experience or intelligence test for voting. But even many voters in their twenties might not pass an "experience" test; and if the professor is allowed to make the *reductio ad absurdum* to football, might we not ask whether an even more stringent "experience" test would be in order—perhaps to exclude all persons under 50!

After all, is not the question of experience really one of ability to learn one's lesson? And if this is so, we must consider the intelligence test as a prerequisite to voting. This is clearly undemocratic, but if it were to be the standard, youth would win out, for young people have more education per capita than any other age group and are more experienced in taking (and passing) examinations.

Statistics from the U.S. Office of Education bear out their superior education level. Twenty years ago about 75 percent of 14-to-17-year-olds were in high school; today the figure is about 95 percent. Twenty years ago slightly over 25 percent of those between 18 and 21 were in college; today the figure is about 50 percent. As a result, an intelligence test might very well disfranchise much of the over-30 population and leave us with a young electorate.

Furthermore, the 18-year-old vote would provide a great opportunity for the political parties to come onto the campus in force, for they might learn a few things. Conversely, students who now feel they must spin off into militant groups might find the regular political apparatus more open to their grievances and needs. That sort of constructive outlet is sorely needed.

Colleges nationwide are beginning to realize that students desperately want to break the hold of *in loco parentis* and that they are prepared to accept the responsibilities and liabilities which would accompany that change. And what is necessarily so corrupting about our political parties that we must protect America's young people from their sinister influence?

In their report the young Republican Congressmen who toured

campuses in 1969 aptly noted: "Between the time they become eligible for the draft, and the time they presently become eligible to vote, there is a natural tendency to lose interest in politics and government because there is no right to participate. An extension of the franchise to the age of 18 when their interest is high can help engender in our youth (and our future leadership) an awareness of the full meaning of democracy."[8] In sum, the activists are already involved in public issues, and many of their more passive friends might take an interest in politics if given the vote.

One final argument against the 18-year-old vote is on the grounds of consistency: Why allow an 18-year-old to vote when he is not old enough to enjoy other legal rights and responsibilities? This is another of Representative Celler's arguments. "Down there [in Georgia, where one may vote at 18] you have many inconsistencies," Celler points out. "They let them vote, but they can't make a contract. They can't have inheritances without guardians. They cannot sell a cow or a mule or a horse; they cannot serve on juries. They cannot do things that we ordinarily have people over 21 do."

All this is true; the law is inconsistent. But this argument does not justify depriving the 18-to-21 age group of *all* rights. We have shown that this group deserves the vote; for the sake of consistency, they should be given other legal rights as well. This is a matter that we shall consider later in this chapter.

OUTLOOK FOR THE 18-YEAR-OLD VOTE

Today there is a nationwide nonpartisan alliance to secure the 18-year-old vote, the Youth Franchise Coalition. Headquartered in Washington, D.C., the YFC is made up of over thirty participating organizations, including such disparate groups as the YMCA, National Student Association, National Education Association, the Americans for Democratic Action, Southern Christian Leadership Conference, NAACP, the Episcopal Church Executive Council, the Young Democrats, and The Ripon Society. It has a long way to go, but it is learning effective lobbying techniques and victory will probably come within the next few years.

It is important to consider what the effects of the 18-year-old vote would be. There are two myths about these effects. One is, in the words of an NEA official, "By taking in this new population of voters we would get some changes in our public officials."[9]

This implies two things: that 18-to-21-year-old voters would add significantly to the voting registers, and that they would vote fairly cohesively. Neither is likely to occur.

First, there are going to be from 10 to 12 million 18-to-21-year-olds in the next few years. If the experience in Alaska, Georgia, Hawaii, and Kentucky, where people under 21 may vote, is relevant, less than 40 percent of this group will actually go to the polls. (This low turnout rate is partly due to the high level of mobility of young people, who have not yet established roots in any community.[10]) This means well under 5 million new voters. Added to a present voting population of about 75 million, those under 21 will account for less than 7 percent of the electorate.

Second, there is no indication that young people are any more likely than their elders to vote as a cohesive bloc. While polls indicate that young people are on the whole more liberal than older people, they are hardly unanimous in their views.

The other general forecast regarding the 18-year-old vote was stated succinctly by Senator Jacob Javits, of New York: "There should be no need for civil disobedience in a political system that meets the needs of its population . . . that guarantees the right of orderly protest and redress of grievances through the ballot box."

But those who expect the vote to be an antidote to the protest movements of the young will be disappointed. Young activists are protesting deep-rooted conditions in our society—racism, militarism, pollution, academic inadequacies—and will not be bought off with a ballot. Giving the 18-year-olds the vote will not destroy these ills, and young people realize it. They can look to the blacks as an example of a group that was given the vote but still lacks equal opportunity in economic and social conditions; the vote will not solve everything. And even adults wonder how meaningful the vote is when political candidates are chosen by machine-dominated conventions and candidates must be wealthy to afford a major campaign.

Other Legal Rights

Again and again the law discriminates against young people, especially those from 18 to 21. Adult demands are made on youth, but adult rights and privileges are often denied them. For example:

The Selective Service System allows 75-year-olds to induct 18-year-olds into service, and even forbids anyone under age 30 to serve on a draft board.

In the courts, a defendant 18 to 21 years old is tried as an adult, but he may not serve on a jury; in practice, few people between 21 and 25 serve on juries.

Soldiers on leave find that, lacking credit, they are not allowed to rent cars. Moreover, like civilians, they must be 25 to rent a car even with credit in many places.

The question may be raised, Why make 18 the cutoff point? The answer is that 18 has become the natural dividing point in life. By that age most young people have graduated from high school and are in the labor force, in college, or in military service.

Even the law recognizes this in some ways. At 16 or 17 a young person may decide for himself whether to stay in school. At 18 he may purchase cigarettes and, in some states, alcoholic beverages. At 18 one is tried in court as an adult. Civil service begins to employ at 18, and in myriad other ways the law considers 18-year-olds "adults."

The entire legal code must be adapted to this reality. For example, there is the marriage right. In most states marriage is allowed for males at 18 and females at 16—an unnecessary and invidious distinction—if there is parental consent; and women cannot marry until 18 without it. However, most states have a judicial procedure by which a minor may marry without parental consent if the court approves. Thus, in practice, hardly anyone is denied the right to marry at 18, if for no other reason than because parents and courts alike realize the futility of trying to restrain them. Over one million 18- and 19-year-olds are married in this country today. Obviously, the next step should be to change the marriage law to reflect the reality that already exists.

The same is true of contracts. Most parents and most merchants are willing to let 18-year-olds enter into contracts; many young people do in fact contract (albeit with parental permission) to buy cars. In some states an 18-year-old may contract for a car even without parental permission if he requires the car for his work. No doubt if all 18-year-olds could contract independently, some would get into financial difficulty. But presumably the same older persons who sign for 20-year-olds now would come to their aid then. Moreover, if an 18-year-old has the legal right to drive an automobile, with all the life-and-death responsibilities that that entails, he should be deemed responsible enough to buy an automobile.

Similarly, the law should be changed to permit young people to serve on juries, especially since they can be tried as adults. If a person of 18 chosen for jury duty is deemed too immature in judgment, the court may dismiss him, just as it may dismiss an older person for that or any other reason.

According to a survey by pollster Louis Harris, "Older people, as befits their traditional status in life, are less tolerant of nonconformity, more opposed to change, more wedded to the status quo . . . Nearly 50 percent more young people than older see the right to dissent as citical to our society."[11] Since the Supreme Court decisions on civil rights and liberties seem to be more accepted by the young than by the old, the persons sitting in the jury boxes should be sensitive to the changing nature of legal interpretations. And since many decisions vitally affect the interests of youth, young people should be represented in these cases.

As for the qualifications set by the legal, medical, and other professions, these are mostly a function of education, not age. Most attorneys do not pass the bar until their mid-twenties, but few would argue for, say, 25 as a qualification. Doctors normally are even older when they complete medical school. If the voting age and other rights are dropped uniformly to 18, then age requirements *per se* will drop in the professions too.

A NATIONAL EFFORT

Lowering the age of majority in America will be an effective recognition of a new voice in the affairs of the nation. Once the legal age of maturity drops, so will other age limitations. The time will come when the Constitution will be revised to eliminate the restrictions that prevent anyone under 35 from running for the

Presidency, under 30 from running for the Senate, and under 25 from running for the House of Representatives. If a person younger than those ages is otherwise qualified for the job, he should be allowed to seek it. (Nine of the signers of the Declaration of Independence, including its author, Thomas Jefferson, were under 35.)

Meanwhile, the President has the moral authority to lead the fight for the vote and other rights for 18-to-21-year-olds. He should submit federal legislation to that effect, and urge the states to do likewise.

Furthermore, the President should appoint a special commission to review all the inconsistencies in present federal and state laws and in common practice, and to recommend whatever reforms are indicated. As a pledge of his concern, the President should appoint at least half its members from the 18-to-30 age group. In addition to the topics touched on here, subjects for the commission's study might include the age at which one may consent to medical treatment, to maintain a separate domicile, to make a will, or to apply for a passport.

At the least such a commission could recommend uniform standards for all states. At the most, it could provide the President with the outline for historic legislation, including a stronger mandate for the 18-year-old vote he already supports.

Legal rights for 18-to-21-year-olds, especially the vote, are essential to healing the breach between the generations. By showing young people that they are considered worthy of trust, by extending to them the blessings of liberty, older Americans will inspire a renewed sense of responsibility.

Chapter 10

YOUTH IN SERVICE

Voluntarism and Government Service

Amid all the news reports of lawlessness and irresponsibility among youth, the cry is heard, "Why don't they ever show the *good* things that young people do?" For there *are* large numbers of young people who tutor schoolchildren, help nurses in hospitals, counsel in summer camps, work in government, and perform other socially useful functions, but these go unnoticed by the media because they are not bizarre or unusual. Young people have always been willing to devote their idealism and energy to humanitarian causes.

In this chapter we will present The Ripon Society's proposal for a National Foundation for Youth Service, as well as some ideas for meaningful programs for government hiring of young people in summer.

Voluntarism in American Life

In recent years young people have tended to be skeptical of government solutions to national life. Indeed, centralization in many forms is a prime target of today's youth. This is not a naive or reactionary desire to deprive the federal government of its necessary functions. As Paul Goodman observes, no one wants decentralized standards of weights and measures or decentralized management of the space program. But American youth are calling for more diversity and experimentation, and their yearning for a more equitable social order tends to make them suspicious of federal nostrums that appease their Depression- and war-conditioned elders.

Decentralization and voluntarism would not mean, as some of the New Left and radical right think, that every man could "do his thing" outside any organization or structure, without leadership or guidance. One cannot combat the dehumanizing features of overcentralization simply by upending the power structure in Washington. Power does not for long remain diffused. Even if it were possible to take away all the power of the central government, that power would drain into some other structure, as it did into business in the late nineteenth century, or, through some circular route, back to a fresh constitution of centralism. The need is for an orderly framework for cooperation and expression of the public interest within decentralization. "Orderly anarchy" is as much a self-contradiction as "the dictatorship of the proletariat."

Today's disharmony in public affairs results from a power imbalance; the central government promotes dehumanizing legalism and rigidity where it imagines it is promoting service. To restore the balance means to invest state and local government, and particularly voluntary associations, with new strength and capabilities. Youth's stake in such a development can hardly be overstated.

The voluntary sector of society certainly does not need to be invented. Innumerable charitable institutions such as the cancer funds and the Red Cross are combating disease and injury and natural disaster; there are 2,000 Community Chests and United Funds alone. Civil-rights organizations such as the Urban League, NAACP, CORE, to name only a few, are responsible for many of the substantial advances in human liberty in the past two decades, and their leadership promises continued progress. The 15,000 private research and philanthropic foundations, whose collective worth is over $15 billion, dispense nearly a billion dollars a year on widely assorted projects. The charitable activities of 118 million members in 320,000 churches raise millions of dollars to benefit the sick and the disadvantaged, and church groups are intensifying their engagement with the problems of urban society.

Add to these 1,357 private colleges and universities; the poverty programs operated by civic groups, labor unions, and businesses; the 3,500 voluntary hospitals; the massive nongovernment youth programs (Boy Scouts, Boys Clubs, Junior Achievement, etc.), the scholarship funds, conservation projects, and civic improvement associations. Certainly the aggregate contribution of volunteer organizations to the public good is beyond measure.

However, the present importance and the potential for dynamic growth of the volunteer sector are little appreciated. Even Congress, which gets much of its information from empire builders in the federal departments, knows little of the volunteer sector's activities. Often groups working in areas in which Congress is planning legislation are not even consulted. Yet not only is the volunteer sector a tremendously significant source of social initiative, it usually is more economical and effective than government. For example, when students at Harvard organize a new community action program, of which they now operate several, there is no red tape in the planning stages, and no bureaucrats to okay experimentation or expansion. Using highly motivated youth as part-time volunteers, such a project—typical of the voluntary sector at its best—costs little in dollars and establishes relationships with the community that are personal and constructive, the seeds for spontaneous cooperation in the future.

On a larger scale, volunteer associations for years have performed humanitarian service abroad, and today 33,000 Americans are working in 146 countries under the sponsorship of such groups. We are all proud of the Peace Corps, a federal program patterned after the International Voluntary Services, a highly successful private group. But the Peace Corps has only 10,000 volunteers, and, as an arm of government, the number of countries served by it varies with the fate of official U.S. relations around the world. Moreover, while it costs $8,000 to train a Peace Corpsman, Volunteers in Service Abroad, an overseas assistance program operated by the Society of Friends, spends only $3,500 to train one of its participants. In short, dollar for dollar, and often man-hour for man-hour, the volunteer sector uses its resources better than government does.

Of course, the volunteer sector has its faults too. Among the most regrettable is the tendency of some of its leaders to see their job as demonstrating the worth of a project so that the federal government will take it over. This attitude, rife in the foundations, totally ignores the value of independence and voluntarism. More-over, the volunteer sector never can grow in power and influence if it dispatches its best ideas to the government. Another failing is that many volunteer organizations, especially those with money to grant, are afraid to involve themselves with political or contro-versial projects, abandoning them either to private economic in-terests or to the government. The case several years ago of the National Student Association and its CIA-financed overseas pro-gram is a classic example of the demoralization that can follow government subvention of activities which the volunteer sector has declined to support.

Other people within the volunteer sector, namely, those who urge National Service, put such value on the service aspects of their activities that they forget the value of voluntarism. They would exploit the draft system to acquire all the manpower the military services don't need—which, even during the present Vietnam war, is a majority of all men. (Dr. Margaret Mead, the noted anthro-pologist, would even include women in National Service, though she wryly declares she would draw the line at military combat "because women are too ferocious.")

National Service simply would extend the inequities of the present draft system and, indeed, complete the corruption of the right to free choice. It also would create a monstrous boondoggle, compounding the inefficiency and cynicism often found in the peacetime military.

It is sometimes said that National Service really would be "vol-untary," because one could opt to take his chances in the draft instead, and because if one did enter National Service he could pick from a long list of government-approved social projects. But that is sophistry; the coercion is still there, not to mention the bias toward centralism.

Many older people favor National Service for youth; few young people do. In fact, it runs contrary to the values most youth seek to restore to society—spontaneity, free choice, tolerance for diversity, individualism.

But the volunteer sector's faults, and the misconception of some of its advocates, are an argument not for its curtailment, but for its expansion. Some further federal innovation is needed, of course, and there is still room for truly voluntary service programs within the federal system. But our most compelling social-service need is for a sweeping program of social action that is citizen-oriented. In particular, we need a whole generation of enlightened citizens dedicated to making it a success.

Those now eighteen to thirty years old may be that generation. Their identification with an older but freshly stated concept of service is the nation's hope of easing the anxieties that plague the exhausted generation now in command and for realizing the opportunities for participatory citizenship only hinted at in the political structures of today.

A Voluntary Program for Youth

A first step in encouraging participation in public service would be an income tax *credit* (as opposed to the present tax *deduction,* which is not very helpful to those with small incomes, such as most young people) for money contributed to charitable or recognized public-service organizations. Another tax credit should be granted for contributions to any political party, political committee, or semipolitical (e.g., civil rights) committee.

The government can well afford the loss of income that would result from these tax credits, limited, as they should be, to a small fraction of one's total tax bill (say, $10 per person a year). The cost of the Vietnam war and the resulting cutback in domestic federal spending have caused many people to overlook the fact that federal revenues are growing by some $7 billion a year; at war's end the loss of a few hundred million to the volunteer sector for public-service purposes will be quite feasible, and in the long run would save the government money.

More controversial, however, would be tax credits for political activities. Many in Congress propose that some financial aid be given directly to the major parties, but outright grants inevitably would entail government controls and ignore the essential role of partisan and bi-partisan groups (the Americans for Democratic Action, the Young Americans for Freedom, The Ripon Society, the National Committee for an Effective Congress, etc.). These organizations and small protest parties would be squeezed out by the two major parties. The two major parties, meanwhile, would remain just as unresponsive as they are now, but with vast, new centralized power. On the other hand, a small tax credit, again limited to $10, for contributions to any political or semipolitical group would leave choice with the individual taxpayer. Though some might give their money to the Black Panthers or to the John Birch Society, just as they give nondeductible money now, others would donate to more "respectable" groups, just as they do now. Everyone would be master of his own contribution, and of course could opt to make no contribution and simply pay the money as taxes. Abuses (fake committees and the like) would be investigated by the Internal Revenue Service, just as abuses are in the present system. It would be a subsidy of no one group; it would be an incentive for all to participate in decision making.

The two proposed tax incentives would stimulate enormous vitality in the voluntary sector. Young people especially would be assisted in acquiring the habit of giving (their tax bracket is usually so low that present *deduction* incentives do not suffice to induce financial participation in charitable and service projects). The volunteer associations would be at once aided and influenced by this new financial constituency. The effect would be greatest on youth-controlled associations, particularly those concerned with politics. These groups would be enormously invigorated by a tax credit that enabled their members for the first time to give money as well as energy to their causes.

Another way in which a youth lobby might help expand the role of voluntarism would be through the creation of a National Foundation for Youth Service, designed to broaden involvement in essentially nonpolitical service and to emphasize the truth that service serves both the served and the server. This would be similar to Bud Wilkinson's National Center for Voluntary Action. Such a foundation could be established by a one-time-only federal endowment, adapted from the formula Lincoln pioneered in founding the land-grant colleges. The endowment principle represents another way the government can pump new life into the volunteer sector, to redress the balance it itself upset, while retaining no management of volunteer programs thereafter. It should get in and get out. Private sources, spurred by the tax incentives recommended earlier, would finance future capital expansion.

Such a foundation would not operate any service projects of its own, but would complement and assist programs already in operation. Most young Americans are unaware of the wide variety of service opportunities available to them. A National Foundation for Youth Service would collect and publish local, regional, and national lists of service positions available, and would function as a clearinghouse for helping the right person find the right project. This activity would be coordinated with high schools and colleges throughout the nation. The foundation also might accumulate and distribute information on paying jobs that have a service aspect to them, such as interning in a mayor's office or counseling at a summer camp. These clearinghouse functions would include both summer projects and projects lasting one or two years after one's formal education.

The foundation would grant a certain number—hopefully many —of service fellowships on a "subsistence-plus" basis to young people, especially the poor, who would like to take a meaningful job with service significance but who have to have some financial assistance in order to afford it. Such service builds confidence, broadens outlook, and enhances skills. More important, a subsidy program would make service opportunities available to rich and poor alike, which unhappily is not now true of many spheres of nongovernment volunteer activity. Surely equality of opportunity to *serve* should be enshrined among the other evolving values of this generation.

Such a program to stimulate service would anticipate a day when a large majority of students would give one or more of their summers or possibly one or two years after their schooling to a humanitarian cause. There are thousands of tasks in America and abroad that want doing, with plenty of choice among them for any individual—hospital work, special projects for retarded children and slum children, church-affiliated programs, beautification projects, overseas assistance. In almost every instance a volunteer program already exists. Where one does not, the volunteer sector always will be more quick, inventive, and experimental than the federal government in devising one. All that's needed is more volunteers.

Since service is a broadening and educational experience, colleges might give credit for certain volunteer projects, just as some do already for Peace Corps service. In an article proposing a mandatory period of national service, Professor Amitai Etzioni, of the Columbia University sociology department, suggests several other incentives. Although his proposal is different from the present one, some of his incentives would be applicable. For example, he urges that colleges make "national service a prerequisite for awarding a fellowship." While we would not go that far, certainly a period of service should be considered when fellowship money is allocated. Professor Etzioni also suggests that governmental and private employers look with favor upon young people with service experience. Furthermore, he notes, voluntary service would afford the student who is undecided about his goals an opportunity to drop out of school for a while without stigma. During his leave of absence he could provide service as well as find himself.[1]

The proposed National Foundation for Youth Service would take action to increase the mobility of service volunteers. A cooperative arrangement with the nation's railroads, airlines, and bus lines could be sought to provide free transportation for any young person participating in a service project away from his home. In Denmark the national railroad gives every secondary-school student a round-trip ticket to any place he chooses to travel during summer vacation. In America the tickets could be limited to youths in service projects.

The arrangement with the rail, air, and bus lines would be optional on their part, possibly encouraged by a tax incentive. A representative of the Santa Fe Railroad told The Ripon Society that space might be granted on a standby-only basis or during non-peak periods of the week, as are certain half-fare youth prices now. But he said that generally the public-relations advantage and the development of the future travel market would be sufficient inducement for the transportation industry to participate. Thus a Harlem student with a summer service job in the Rockies could have a way to get to it, while in another case the ticket would mitigate the loss of earnings for a middle-class student from California who took a volunteer teaching job on Chicago's South Side.

Toward the same end, the foundation might stimulate the youth-hostel program in this country. In Europe students and other young persons can visit great cities, parklands, and historic sites for very little money while staying at clean and respectable youth hostels run by churches, the government, and other nonprofit institutions. The hostels usually charge less than a dollar a night for room and board. In America, however, the hostel program lacks adequate funding, and young people are frequently faced with a choice of an expensive hotel or a flophouse. A properly financed national system of youth hostels, perhaps operated in connection with our universities and churches, would complement the service scholarship and travel programs and further encourage fellowship among youth of many backgrounds.

Another, wholly different kind of volunteer program can be run by universities located in or near inner-city ghetto areas. Certainly it would be very beneficial to the communities, to the students, and to university-community relations for the university to establish service centers that can be manned by student volunteers. An added incentive to the young people might be academic credits for volunteer work related to their field of major study.

It does not take much imagination to realize how students can be useful in community service. Those who lack specialized professional training can be medical aides, tutors and adult-education teachers, welfare caseworker aides, recreation supervisors, and staffers of day-care centers. Graduate students can be even more useful, in medical programs, education, social work, and legal aid. Students who seek meaningful political experience can participate in community organizing. Others whose skills are administrative can help run the service centers.

The federal government has already helped to sponsor this kind of university/community cooperation through Title I of the Higher Education Act of 1965. Fairleigh Dickinson (Newark), the University of Buffalo, Temple (Philadelphia), Virginia State College (Norfolk), North Carolina College (Durham), Southern (New

Orleans), Minnesota (Minneapolis), Washington (St. Louis), and U.C.L.A. are among the schools that have participated in such federally aided programs.

A number of worthy programs utilizing volunteers are operated by the government itself, and for the sake of diversity, these should be continued. Moreover, as President Nixon said in his 1968 campaign, these activities should be brought together under one independent youth service agency in the administration. This organization also would contain a sports and fitness section, a world activity section, and "a young people's ombudsman."

But most of the government's attention should go to encouraging volunteer projects outside the federal system. The ruling guide should be: Support the idea of service, but leave it unbound. Above all, allow youth the greatest chance to reassert this venerable American virtue, to give it renewed meaning.

TOWARD MORE MEANINGFUL GOVERNMENT SERVICE

Each summer thousands of young men and women converge on Washington, D.C., and other centers of government to fill jobs open to students. The philosophy of these programs is sound: They provide employment for the young, often a valuable part of their educational and vocational experience, and additional help for government agencies at a time when employees are taking vacations.

In recent years, however, budget cuts in Washington and elsewhere have reduced these vital programs. Perhaps most disgraceful was the action of the House of Representatives in destroying its own summer intern program in 1968 because during the previous summer several interns had circulated a petition against the war in Vietnam. We may well wonder what kind of citizenship these young people were supposed to learn, if they could not even petition their government for a redress of grievances without retaliation from the people's representatives.

The most plentiful summer jobs in the federal government are in the many executive-branch agencies. There, summer employees fall into three categories: economically disadvantaged teenagers, undergraduates, and graduate students. The disadvantaged teenagers are hired under a program entitled the Youth Opportunity Corps (YOC). They are paid extremely low wages and, more often than not, are given menial tasks. Assigned to an office, a young woman might do nothing more enlightening than running a copying machine; assigned to a research laboratory, a young man may do nothing more stimulating than cleaning animal cages.

Too often government employees assigned to supervise the YOC employees fall into stereotyped thinking about the capacities of the poor and the young. It may never occur to a typist that the YOC girl in the office can be taught typing or other valuable office skills when the work load allows for a little time off; a scientist may not realize that the boy who cleans the cages may be able to handle some fairly sophisticated lab technique. Even a stock clerk can be shown how the books are kept. Certainly for the YOCs, by definition economically disadvantaged, there can be no better gift than a marketable skill (and a badly needed raise in pay would help too).

The college students hired by the government are also given jobs far below their level of competence. Frequently a student who may have gotten all A's in political science finds himself filing memos or running a duplicating machine.

Of course, the average office cannot assign each of its employees a job of high responsibility. But supervisors should at least make the effort to give the employees a general working knowledge of the agency and allow them to attend staff meetings to see how government works. Many agencies that deal with the affairs of youth would do well to follow the example of Commissioner of Education Harold Howe II, who decided in 1968 that the Office of Education has a valuable resource in its college employees and began to use this body of workers as a springboard for new ideas about higher-education programs.

The government is especially interested in hiring graduate students, in the hope that these individuals will be attracted to government service as a permanent occupation, and thus it is imperative that they be given jobs commensurate with their skills. Since the best young government employees are hired under the management intern program, it seems sensible to allow a summer-

time graduate-student employee to accumulate credit for his work
that can be used in determining his job and pay when and if he
becomes a management intern.

Improvements can be made across the board with regard to all
summer employees. Every state and local government should adopt
a summer hiring program along the lines of the federal program,
including legislative aides. The federal government should give
high priority to its program, for if in the future the number of
talented people entering government service drops, it will be due
in part to the severely limited opportunities for students to be
introduced to government early in life, and to learn how reforms
can be enacted without the need for confrontation.

A second general improvement would be to combine government employment with community-service projects. For example,
government agencies could contact local projects which need volunteers and publicize these activities among the summer interns.
Perhaps an even more ambitious approach could be taken: The
government could contact high schools, colleges, and graduate
schools and offer to hire students for the summer if they agree to
combine their work with community service.

Schools could even provide educational background for such
integrated programs. For instance, a state welfare agency might
contact a college and offer to hire a group of students for the summer if they would agree to do voluntary community service in
their off-hours. Before the summer began, the college social-science
departments could offer seminars or reading lists to these students
and prepare them for some of the issues faced by welfare agencies.
During the summer the students would work after hours at day-
care centers, with caseworkers, and at other activities related to
welfare. They would not only be providing talent to both the government and community, but their educational experience would
be three-dimensional (school, government, and voluntarism).

A NEW APPROACH

In a meeting with President Nixon at the White House, members of The Ripon Society suggested that the government could
utilize the talents of the best of our nation's youth by inviting

them to Washington in the summer to observe the bureaucracy and propose changes in policy areas of special interest to young people. The President expressed great interest in the idea, and so a new approach to government service was born.

The plan is to have a number of task forces of several students each, and a project leader to coordinate activity and direct research. The purpose of the task forces is to open government up to the public view, to give the agencies the benefit of fresh perspectives, and to engage young people directly in projects where their views can have an effect. Advisers from the administration and from private institutions are to work with the task forces to ensure that government agencies provide full cooperation and to give task-force members the benefit of their experience and expertise.

Each task force is to be oriented in one of two directions—toward evaluation of government performance in a particular area, or toward development of new policies—and each will work to align public policy with new perspectives and to increase government's capacity to handle today's problems.

The initial number of task forces is to be modest, because of the experimental nature of the program. One likely project is population policy; the task force would evaluate the effects, direct and indirect, of all government programs on the birth rate, with the aim of establishing a framework for a coherent national population policy. Another task force might be concerned with ways to implement a volunteer arm, an item of high priority on the President's list. A third topic could be voluntary service, the task force trying to implement the kinds of ideas expressed in the first part of this chapter and focusing a critical eye on present government volunteer programs such as the Peace Corps and VISTA.

Finally, a fruitful topic would be implementation of the "open Presidency," a campaign promise of President Nixon and the inspiration for this entire program. The task force would consider how communications between the President and disaffected Americans (especially young Americans) can be improved.

In Service to America

Surely a nation that cannot utilize the creative talents of its people is a nation in danger of stagnation. Young people have always exhibited a willingness to volunteer service to others and to their government; they rise to this challenge. But in a complex society the individual often feels lost; he does not know where to turn to offer his services. Only by following the initiatives proposed on these pages can we channel the resources of bright, hard-working young people into service for their fellow man in a way that not only our nation, not only those who receive services, but also the young volunteers themselves will reap great rewards.

Chapter 11

EDUCATION POLICY

Toward Relevance in Higher Education

*Most of this book is written from the viewpoint of young people themselves. Here, we present some ideas of two officials of the U.S. Department of Health, Education, and Welfare to show how government can respond to the needs of America's youth.—*ED.

Federal thinking about youth and higher education during the 1960s focused primarily on the problem of access. College was deemed to be a good thing which the federal government should make available to the poor as well as the rich, and so government helped meet this demand by subsidizing construction programs, books, and numbers of teachers. But few federal officials gave much thought to what was going on *inside* the colleges, between students and teachers. Hence when students began to charge that higher education was not "relevant" to their needs and interests, they raised unsettling questions in Washington: How directly should the federal government get mixed up with the *content* of higher education? What could the government do?

The issue of federal involvement at first turned on how to still the chants of "On strike, shut it down" and punish those wo dared act out such anger. For a change, it was the "conservatives" who had to build majority coalitions in an effort to pass new (repressive) legislation and the "liberals" who could snipe at these efforts from bastions of minority strength. The result of the first battles, by and large, was a victory for those who wished to avoid having the government assume the role of campus cops.

Yet all the underlying issues of the "crisis of relevance" in

American higher education remain, and in some cases are becoming more serious. In the 1970s the government will have to be increasingly concerned about the kind of educational experience young people are having in college. Relevance, of course, is not the only objective toward which a federal policy for higher education must be aimed, but it is one the government will be unable to avoid. If this issue were well in hand, everyone would surely breathe a good deal easier.

The difficulty is that we do not know what students mean by "relevance." It seems clear that the term means different things to different people, but the conclusion is the same: Things as they are are unsatisfactory. This consensus might provide the basis for policy changes to avert disaster, but it is not very helpful for diagnosing what specifically is wrong with the system, or in what directions changes should occur.

It is possible, however, to make some guesses about what is wrong. Teachers who hold classes but do not teach are on everyone's list. Sheer neglect of students by faculty is a problem, but surely a diagnosis of what is wrong must go deeper than this and involve the students too. Unhappily, problems of relevance would probably remain even if we filled the system with willing teachers, for any educational experience will be relevant to a student only if he has some sense of where he is going. Yet many students today, it seems, are so unsure about their lives that they lack the criteria necessary for making choices.

The entire educational system compounds this problem by insulating young people from the kinds of experiences that would put them into contact with varieties of careers and life-styles. The majority of students in college today entered school when they were five and proceeded grade by grade to college with breaks only for summer vacation. They have seen lots of teachers, but not much of the world. At some point in college young people must choose to major in a subject that will be relevant to their careers and interests. Understandably, the decision is often an unsettling one, and the choice arbitrary.

What is wrong with American education might therefore be traced to two facts: that school has played too inclusive a role in the lives of many young people and that it comes all at once, rather than at times when study can be most advantageously enjoyed and used. (Many teachers report that the servicemen who returned to college on the GI bill after World War II were the best students they had, which lends some support to this view.) Young people themselves, of course, can hardly be blamed for not bucking the system, given the extent to which our society relies on high-school and college credentials. If many students (as Kingman Brewster has been saying) are in fact involuntary students, going through the motions of schooling in order to receive the necessary credentials for mobility, it is society at large that must be held accountable.

Surely things are wrong inside the schools. If we look at the collective aspirations of those who run our colleges and universities, for most it is Harvard or bust. Status accrues to universities that act like Harvard, to colleges that act like universities, and to community colleges that act like private colleges. This is not to say that Harvard is not a great place for Harvard students (though this might be debated); but the way Harvard educates its students is not necessarily appropriate for every other person who wants a college education. Yet somehow we have decided, or assumed without deciding, that sitting behind a desk listening to a learned professor is *the* way education happens.

If one dominant model for all higher education is inappropriate now, it will be even more so in the future. When statisticians are revealing that there will be six college students in 1975 for every five today, discussion tends to focus on where the students will be stored. How will so many be educated? At present fully a quarter of our college students are in institutions of over 20,000, and the trend is upward.

The real challenge of the 1970s will be, not accommodating the additional students, but adjusting to them. By and large, they will be young people whose parents did not attend college; many will be from disadvantaged families, and can be expected to have a difficult time viewing themselves as college students. With the enrollment increases will come the need for different kinds of education than we have known before. To deliver on a commitment to provide equality of opportunity, we will have to provide each student with not just an admissions ticket but also with an equal chance to profit from his stay in college.

Moreover, even middle-class students will need educational experiences more stimulating than those of the past. We may reject the demands for courses in astrology and revolutionary tactics, but youth's insistence on a vital reconstruction of the educational process cannot be ignored. It is possible for education to be made exciting, but new approaches are sometimes expensive. The dreary is cheap, and the tolerance of boredom displayed by students in the past has helped the development of universities, much as cheap labor helps build a nation. But that tolerance appears to be at an end.

Relevance raises other problems too, but these will do for starters. The point is that we are living in an era of dramatic social change and our system of higher education will have to change very fast just to keep pace.

SOME DREAMS

In government, planning for change is frequently and unavoidably a slow process. One assumes a given market or system (housing, transportation, education), gauges the drift of public needs and tastes, and considers how the system can be adjusted with the federal leverage at hand. Such scientific method is of no avail, however, when the demands on the market or system are changing radically, as when a nation shifts from a wartime to a peacetime economy. There is then a necessity to imagine what one would do starting from scratch. Let us suppose, therefore, there were no such thing as formal higher education in the United States, that the present 7 million students as well as the faculty and deans were doing other things.

Without the knowledge and options college brings, young people would undoubtedly have a hard time finding their way around our complex society. There would be much less opportunity for individuals to advance in terms of social class. Yet in a society without dropouts, distinctions between degree holders and between B.A.s and A.A.s, between Harvard men and graduates of teachers colleges, many young people would be happier and better adjusted.

Employers would have to devise their own tests for hiring rather than relying on the verdict of academicians, and quite a few young people would find they could beat this system better than the existing one. Career choices would come earlier and would probably be more permanent even if mistaken. Job satisfaction, for many, might be greater than at present.

Without a predetermined time and place for learning, young people would have to be responsible for their own education. Society, of course, would have a stake in seeing to it that knowledge was successfully passed on from generation to generation. Apprenticeships might be expanded. Museums, libraries, theaters, and television might assume much of the burden of cultural education.

For advanced knowledge too difficult to learn through apprenticeships, some type of formal education would have to be available, but this we would try to do without altering the individual's feeling that he would be free to choose *not* to go to college. Equality of opportunity should not depend on a status symbol. Hence in designing our system of higher education we would hold a very expanded notion of what higher education might involve. We would design not only institutions in the traditional mold of colleges and universities, but also others modeled after the Peace Corps, the Civilian Conservation Corps, the RAND Corporation, the White House Fellows program, business and professional internships, and Fulbright grants abroad and at home. There would be institutions that separate or combine educational functions in new ways; professional institutes in which a student could move from high school directly into training for law, medicine, or other specializations; research colleges where there would be no student-faculty distinctions; urban-based versions of the Stanford overseas program; and a number of structured, non-college learning opportunities.

College, for those who wanted it, would be available at any time in life. Some would move in lock step as they do now through high school and college; women especially might want to complete the preliminary work of their higher education before taking on the responsibilities of raising a family, so that they could move directly into advanced or professional education when these responsibilities diminished. Many men might want to try out a career before entering or at least before finishing college. Thus colleges would not reinforce the age-segregated character of our society but would encourage individuals of all ages and backgrounds to learn together. In a sense, there would be no alumni—only continuing students.

Starting afresh, we would be able to develop new faculties and concepts of what functions a college should perform. Technology would free us from the notion that a college is a physical place. We would have colleges of the air that would be integrated via commuting; faculties would travel to students as well as the other way around. The institutions would be models of efficiency, operating on a year-round basis; schedules would not be determined by the seasons of the year. Buildings generally would be built more cheaply for temporary use and designed to serve each college's specific mission. Performance tests (for both institutions and students) would place a premium on rapid self-development and provide alternative routes for being credentialed.

SOME REALITIES

It might be thought that some such millennial vision of higher education should become the goal of federal policy and be pursued doggedly until it is achieved. Indeed, unless federal policy is informed by *some* vision of what the overall educational system should look like, specific interventions for narrower purposes will add up to simply meddling. Yet to pronounce such an enormous goal as national policy would be misleading, for it would suggest that the federal role in education can be compared to putting a man on the moon—a misleading comparison. For one thing, it is difficult to visualize a national interest in higher education as cohesive as the interest in landing a man on the moon. There is no consensus on what higher education is for, nor on how much higher education we should buy for our citizens. Neither is there agreement on who should sponsor the higher-education "moon shot." Historically we have tended as a nation to let the government get into the higher-education business only when it seemed absolutely necessary for reasons of defense. The GI bills of World War II and the Korean War, and the federal research support which began during World War II and which increased after Sputnik, were justified in military terms. In the late 1950s when we finally decided that increased federal support was needed for economic reasons, government officials still felt it necessary to label the new programs as the National Defense Education Act.

The decade of the 1960s produced a new consensus that, defense aside, it was good business for the government to invest in higher education. Providing a youngster with the means to get a college degree produced a good return in terms of productivity and taxes. It seemed to make as much sense to provide grants and loans to students and aid to colleges as it did to invest in the oil business. Yet while these economic arguments provided compelling reasons for a federal role in education, they did not still opposition to direct meddling.

In summary, we have allowed the government to finance logistical support for educational trips, and most of us are now agreed that it's all right if the government pays for the admission tickets. But if the government attempts to set the itinerary or take away a ticket from a student who misbehaves, there will be controversy— and so there should be.

Moreover, it is actually much easier to accomplish an Apollo mission than an educational program: It is easier to set performance standards for hardware than for people. We know that excellent teachers are possible, just as we know that excellent computers are possible; but one cannot be bought and the other can. Good teachers are perhaps born rather than made; certainly they cannot be produced routinely by any graduate school existing or imaginable. Federal policy in education must make realistic allowances for the shortage of genius, for dedication that goes on holiday, for human perversity that builds bad academic empires and destroys good ones. Nothing the federal government can do will make academic quality just a matter of good management.

A model of government intervention that would make more sense for higher education is the agricultural programs of the last forty years. They were not designed to make every barnyard a garden of delight, but to encourage innovation, improve marketing, and pass on the benefits of greater productivity to both farmers and consumers. They have sought to balance claims rather than to adjudicate final equities. The agricultural programs have been conspicuously successful where they have given scope to the economic and social motivations of the farmers themselves, and where they have been adaptable to the greatest variety of "human factors," as in the agricultural extension programs. They have done less well on long-range forecasting (e.g., the ecological consequences of insecticides) and social concerns (e.g., the welfare of migrant workers). On balance, the record of federal intervention rates a grade somewhere between a B-plus and a C-minus according to one's point of view, but an A-plus could never have been reasonably expected.

So with federal policy in higher education. The government can forestall crises arising from a shortage of qualified teachers or inadequate facilities. It can guarantee that students have access to loans. It can found new institutions; however, this is unlikely, given the opposition to such a task and the freedom allowed local government and private groups to do so. It can define and test new educational programs just as it developed new strains of wheat, and it can help disseminate these innovations throughout the land. It can also seek to minimize the consequences of its own past mistakes.

A policy framed in these terms might not be modest in its costs, but it must certainly be modest in its assumptions about the engineerability of human behavior. It must avoid assuming genius or complete altruism in the case of any party to the educational enterprise—students, faculty, administrators, state legislators, parents, employers. It could also be a hedge against the failure of the system to respond. The government could offer incentives to faculty to do less research and more teaching, just as it offers incentives to farmers to do less planting and more cultivating; what it must not do is assume that farmers or faculty members respond to economic incentives alone.

WHAT MIGHT WORK

What the federal government might do with a fair chance of success is to try to make the educational system more accountable.

There is not much question that colleges are hardly accountable at all in terms of their stated educational goals. They are perhaps accountable enough to their governing bodies (though few boards of trustees would agree). They are also reasonably accountable in matters amenable to conventional audit. But the institutions are not accountable for the performance of their educational mission. Virtually the only punishment for educating undergraduates badly is the risk that, at some time in the future, so many bright applicants for college admission will have gotten the word that fewer and fewer will want to apply. This is surely the mildest of deterrents.

Indeed, one reason why research has tended to crowd out teaching as a claim on the professors' time is precisely the researcher's greater accountability. The biochemist who fails to find a cure for cancer is not shot to encourage others, but if his papers are few and trivial he will have a harder time getting a grant and getting promoted, not to mention securing attractive offers from universities elsewhere. A reputation as a good teacher gains much less currency among one's peers, is much less negotiable, and is therefore much less worth having.

How then might we make teachers more accountable to students? One obvious answer is to reward exemplary teaching as we reward exemplary research. Yet even if good teachers were given high salaries, Nobel Prizes, and per diems to lecture in Paris—or even just a good secretary and a little more time to rest—most problems would remain. Stodgy professors would not be suddenly transformed into swingers, nor would indifferent instructors begin holding long office hours for students. But such incentives might recruit a few more energetic people into the teaching profession and bring out the potential of those in the system. And they would provide a compensation for the federally financed research prestige system that now rules the land.

Bribes for good teaching, however, while they may remind teachers of their mission, still do not make them accountable to students. For this, students themselves would need to control the resources that faculties need. And it is precisely this fact that economists have cited recently to argue that federal support for higher education should be given increasingly in the form of aid to students rather than to institutions. Let the consumer be king, they say; let the faculty and administration be responsive to the free market of student choices.

There are no guarantees that such a strategy will work. Students are not always intelligent consumers, nor do colleges always provide completely honest information about themselves. What makes the idea of channeling federal aid through students so appealing as a response to their cries for relevance is precisely its simplicity and its modesty. By providing more federal support via aid to students, and thereby making education a buyer's market, we will be encouraging colleges to listen harder. Many sacrosanct institutions will no longer rest on their laurels; they will be made to bear the scrutiny of their students.

Perhaps some day in some place every student's vision of relevance can be realized: a place where mixed-media are used to teach ancient languages, or where botany classes are held on a mountain hillside, or where ghetto English is the language of instruction in pharmacy. But until such a day, students should be given the financial means to choose a college now selling what they really want to buy. Additional financial mechanisms to translate new ideas into new institutions may also be needed. The pity, of course, is that in so many colleges the nineteenth century lives on, and administrators remain oblivious to the huge expansion of higher education in the last twenty years and its potential to offer new vistas.

Chapter 12

DRUG POLICY

To Reform Marijuana Laws

Today our country is undergoing a number of revolutions: the sexual revolution, the fashion revolution, the communications revolution, and perhaps most divisive of all, the drug revolution. Nothing creates a clearer demarcation of the generation gap than the use of drugs. We can see the new widespread drug use everywhere, in popular songs like "White Rabbit" and "Lucy in the Sky," in slanguage such as "turn on," "trip," "bummer," and "joint," in movies like *Easy Rider, Yellow Submarine,* and *2001.*

The chief concern of this chapter will be a weed, *Cannabis sativa,* or marijuana. Marijuana is a species of the hemp family and is the kind of weed that is a gardener's nightmare, extremely hardy and strangely repellant to insects. It grows wild in many parts of the United States, especially in the South and the Midwest. In recent years it has been clandestinely grown in flower boxes in Manhattan, in cellars in New England, and in backyards in California. Occasionally it has appeared in such unexpected places as on the front lawn of a college president's mansion and in the New York sewer system.

This weed has created a national phenomenon, caused an agonizing national self-appraisal, and presented a legal and moral dilemma for which there is no easy answer.

VOICES PRO AND CON

Harry Anslinger, former commissioner of the Federal Narcotics Bureau:
    The marijuana user is a violent criminal, with an insatiable appetite for rape, homicide and mayhem. Eventually it [mari-

juana] renders the user totally insane.[1] (In a statement to Congress in 1937.)

Columnist Joseph Alsop:

Legalize pot and you avoid the kind of monstrosities prohibition ended by producing. For my own part I wish pot had never been heard of, but wishfulness, alas, is always the mother of the worst national follies. It seems to me it is wishful not to face the facts about pot, and to refuse to deal with those facts in a hard practical manner—by legalization under sensible safeguards.[2]

G. Joseph Tauro, Massachusetts superior court justice:

Many succumb to the drug as a handy means of withdrawing from the inevitable stresses and legitimate demands of society. The evasion of problems and escape from reality seem to be among the desired effects of the use of marijuana. Its use is not so much a symbol of dissent in order to effectuate change in our social system, but rather a manifestation of a selfish withdrawal from society. The lessons of history and the experiences of other nations teach us that such artificial alteration of the normal brain function by the use of drugs has been harmful both to the individual and to society in which he lives.[3]

Dr. Stanley Yolles, director of the National Institute of Mental Health:

I know of no clearer instance in which the punishment for an infraction of the law is more harmful than the crime [marijuana use]. I am convinced that the social and psychological damage caused by incarceration is in many cases far greater to the individual and to society than was the offense itself.[4]

Andrew Garvin, twenty-one-year-old *Newsweek* correspondent:

Now, it [marijuana smoking] may be an occasional, pleasant diversion, physically provocative and esthetically rewarding. But smoking grass did not alter the course of my life or uproot my mind. It is simply a casual facet of existence, comparable to other engaging distractions such as skiing.[5]

Joe, a sixteen-year-old high school sophomore:

I started using drugs when I was twelve and a half. At first I just smoked grass, but then some of my friends told me I was square unless I tried speed, so I did, and I liked it. By the time I was fifteen I had shot heroin, something I had promised myself I would never do. I took drugs for a couple of reasons, mostly because it was the thing to do and I wanted people to like me, but also because I was having trouble getting along at home, and drugs give you a warm kind of feeling, sort of like finding a home.

THE PREVALENCE OF MARIJUANA SMOKING

There are no less than 12 million felons walking the streets of the United States today, and the figure is probably much closer to 20 million (10 percent of the total population). They are felons because they have smoked marijuana. Marijuana use is heavily concentrated in the ten-to-thirty age group. It is very likely that 90 percent of the users belong to the 68 million Americans between those ages, and therefore drug use may be as extensive as 35 percent in this age group. An October, 1969, Gallup pool, however, showed that only 4 percent of *adult* Americans had tried marijuana, and 12 percent of those were in their twenties.

Use on college campuses varies widely, with greatest use usually found on the nation's most prestigious campuses such as Harvard and the University of California at Berkeley, and lowest use found on the campuses of the Catholic universities, and universities of the Deep South and the Midwest. A recent survey showed that 38 percent of all American college students have smoked marijuana.[6] At Harvard, studies conducted by outside pollsters, the faculty, and the students themselves all conclude that use exceeds 50 percent. In a survey of students at the Columbia University Law School 69 percent of those who responded to a campus poll replied that they had smoked marijuana at least once (the significance of this survey is diluted by the 60 percent response; it is difficult to estimate the status of the 40 percent who didn't respond).[7] In discussions about marijuana use at Yale, psychologist Kenneth Keniston suggested that drug use was at least as excessive among the best students as it was among the mediocre students.[8] Nearly half the students at the University of Michigan have smoked marijuana.[9] New campus surveys are being made public almost weekly now and they all reveal that marijuana use is heavy among our student population and that it is increasing.

It is more difficult to get a handle on the use of prohibited drugs among high school kids and grade-school children, but it is known that here too violation of drug laws is flagrant, especially in the heavily populated sections of the Northeast and California. *News-week* estimates that as many as one-half of American high school students have tried a variety of drugs.[10] An article in the *Wall Street Journal* revealed the disturbing statistic that in one California high school 342 students have been expelled for marijuana use in the past two years. The article also mentioned that some school districts were so concerned that they were considering giving blood and urine tests to students to check for drug use. These plans were abandoned when the American Civil Liberties Union challenged the legality of the tests, and when it was discovered that neither marijuana nor LSD use could be detected in such tests.[11]

Unbelievable as it may seem, thirteen- and fourteen-year-olds are among the frequent users of marijuana. It may be this fact as much as anything else that has caused President Nixon to reconsider our present drug statutes. At a conference with forty of the nation's governors in December, 1969, President Nixon stated, "When you are talking about 13-year-olds and 14-year-olds and 15-year-olds, the answer is not more penalties. The answer is information. The answer is understanding."

In colleges drug use is largely limited to marijuana. There are exceptions, of course, but it is safe to say that most students are mature enough to know that marijuana at least can be controlled and will not cause permanent impairment.

Unfortunately such is not the case in high schools and junior high schools. Fourteen-year-olds do not spend a lot of time worrying about the future. They are concerned about now, and now for a fourteen-year-old is being one of the gang, being liked by his peers. The horrible part about the whole drug question is that throughout the country, not just in the Northeast and California but in Iowa, Idaho, and North Carolina, it is becoming more and more the norm of the teenage set to be taking drugs.

Father Bernard Lane, a Catholic priest in a Boston suburb, has established a sort of halfway house for young drug takers and he speaks with authority on the subject, having walked the streets and gained the respect of the youngsters the hard way. He suggests that marijuana is usually the way young people get started on hard drugs, but not always. Although he recognizes that marijuana can be controlled by a mature adult, he suggests that any adolescent who makes the leap to try marijuana and thus breaks the law will almost inevitably move on to harder things when he is offered them by his friends.

Father Lane's major point is that drugs are only a symptom of a problem. The problem is that anyone in his early teens is very confused and is seeking to build a value system. He does not yet know how to cope with life, nor does he know where to turn for the answers. At home he sees a pill as a solution to almost every problem from insomnia to headache pain. He sees affluence to the extent that all needs can be satisfied with a credit card. His parents are all too often difficult to communicate with, reluctant to demonstrate the love that they feel for their children, unwilling to show their emotions.

When a youngster comes to his family with the comment that some of his friends are smoking marijuana at school, parents often do not recognize this as a warning. They are apt to retort, "Don't let me ever catch you doing something like that or I'll fix you good." President Nixon wisely noted in his December 1969 statement that education is the key, but it is much more than education of young people. It means education of parents, of teachers, and of the whole society. The drug question is symptomatic of a sociological problem that can only be solved over a period of many years.

RESEARCH IS INCONCLUSIVE

It is time to face the realities of drug research. No amount of it is going to prove to anybody's satisfaction that marijuana is harmless for all people who use it, but neither is it ever likely to prove that marijuana is harmful for most people who use it. No matter how many studies are done, the data will remain inconclusive, ambiguous, and essentially political.

There is a temptation in government today to support drug research that comes up with damning information. This bias is to be avoided at all costs, not only because it seriously compromises the intellectual freedom of scientists, but also because it always turns out to be a bad tactical error.

The scare over the connection between LSD and chromosomes is a case in point. Controlled research has now shown that no significant relationship exists between LSD consumption and chromosomal damage in humans.[12] Many of the original investigators who postulated such a relationship were motivated by genuine concern about LSD abuse, but their zeal led them to overlook basic scientific safeguards against drawing erroneous conclusions. The alacrity of government officials and the press (both scientific and popular) in seizing upon and disseminating these initial conclusions transformed a scientific blunder into a debacle. Overnight it established a credibility gap between drug experts and youth that is probably irreparable. Young drug takers just do not believe what anyone in authority tells them about drugs any more.

Studies of the use and effects of cannabis (the active ingredient in marijuana and hashish) have been made throughout the world for many years, including studies in France, the Middle East, and India at the end of the nineteenth century. Several investigations have also been conducted recently in the United States under grants from the National Institute of Mental Health. The conclusions are contradictory on many of the details, but preliminary findings suggest the following: [13]

That marijuana is not a narcotic and is not physically addictive, as drugs like heroin and cocaine have proven to be. It is possible that marijuana may be psychologically addictive, just as prescriptioned sugar pills may be psychologically addictive. This should not be taken lightly, because a psychological addiction can be as difficult to overcome as a physical one. A patient who has become addicted to heroin when used as a pain killer finds it much easier to break the habit than an escape-seeking addict who has developed a psychological dependence as well.

That the physical effect of marijuana use in the mild form has three symptoms. First, there is an effect on memory and the ability to concentrate. A person high on marijuana might have a great deal of difficulty following the plot of a movie or a television show. He forgets what he has just seen, although marijuana does not create anything approaching advanced forms of memory impairment such as amnesia. Second, marijuana affects the person's concept of time. For example, a three-minute popular song may seem interminable to someone under the influence. Third, marijuana use deepens the senses of smell, feeling, seeing, and hearing. For example, a person high on marijuana can become fascinated by shadows that he had never noticed before in a room.

That marijuana, unlike alcohol, does not cause reckless driving. In fact, it tends to make drivers much more cautious rather than more aggressive.

That because of the expansion of the user's concept of time and the heightening of his senses, marijuana is said to make love making considerably more pleasurable. However, it is not an aphrodisiac.

That under no circumstances has it been shown that marijuana use stimulates criminal behavior (aside from the fact, of course, that its very use is illegal).

THE LEGAL SITUATION

The federal statute that is used to prosecute marijuana users is the Marijuana Tax Act, which requires all transactions involving marijuana to be registered with the federal government in order that a tax may be paid on the sale. At the same time, possession of marijuana is illegal under state laws in all fifty states. The penalties vary widely from state to state, however, and in some states the minimum sentence for first offenders is two years. On May 19, 1969, the Marijuana Tax Act was declared unconstitutional by the U.S. Supreme Court in the case *U.S. vs. Leary*. However, in December 1969 the Supreme Court ruled that peddlers of marijuana may legally be required to obtain official forms from the government prior to sale, and thus incriminate themselves.

Problems with present marijuana statutes go far beyond the problems of a poorly written federal law which relies on a contrivance for prosecution. The laws of the individual states constitute a jungle of widely varying penalties, all of which are by the states' own admission too high. It has been a simple matter for proponents of more lenient statutes to find cases that typify the injustices that the present laws have caused. There is the oft-cited example of a college student who served as an intermediary to purchase marijuana for several of his friends, expecting to gain no profit from the transaction, and was sentenced to a twenty-year prison term in the state of Virginia. Dr. Joel Forte, in an article in *Playboy,* cited the example of a shoe-shine operator in Texas who sold $5 worth of marijuana to an undercover policeman and subsequently was sentenced to fifty years.[14]

There are abundant cases of reputable young people, including children of governors and U.S. Senators, who were caught with small amounts of marijuana. Some judges recognize the need not to ruin a young person's life and will suspend their sentences. But the offenders later discover that jobs are hard to find when their record contains a conviction on a felony charge.

One girl discovered that a person can suffer a similar fate just by being in the presence of marijuana. She discovered too late that her date had a few cigarettes in his pocket and found herself implicated when he was arrested, even though she had no intention of smoking them. She too has been branded an outcast because it is a crime to be an innocent bystander under the statutes of many states. Legal penalties have also been suffered by people who loaned their homes to friends for a pot party, even though they were absent at the time. It is an interesting paradox that the penalty for possession of marijuana is considerably stiffer than the penalty for possession of mescaline and many other much more potent drugs.

Not only are the laws open to question, but the zeal with which they are enforced goes beyond all reason. Use of undercover agents, informers, blank warrants, wiretapping, and other questionable tactics is commonplace. Worst of all is the "No Knock" rule that recently received a favorable airing in Congress.

It is only a matter of time before sweeping reforms will be undertaken to modernize the marijuana statutes, both state and federal, but before this is done it is essential that careful consideration be given to the alternatives facing our lawmakers and that a full understanding of the present situation be reached, especially as it affects youth. Today's teenagers will be responsible for running the country someday, and perhaps Timothy Leary's prediction that Supreme Court justices will be marijuana smokers in fifteen years is fully realistic. After all, public figures as far to the right as William F. Buckley, Jr., have admitted smoking it.[15]

In a November, 1969, report of the Eisenhower Commission on the Causes and Prevention of Violence the following statement was made attacking the essence of the existing problem:

> The startling recent increase in marijuana use by many young people has intensified the conflict between generations and posed enormous problems in the enforcement of drug laws . . .
>
> This patchwork of Federal and state laws, inconsistent and often unenforceable, on its merits has led to an essentially irrational situation. Since many of our youths believe marijuana to be relatively harmless and yet are faced with legal sanctions, they are led into a practice of law evasion which contributes to general disrespect for the law. The situation is reminiscent of problems encountered in enforcement of prohibition during the 1920's.

On the nationally televised show *The Advocates,* anthropologist Margaret Mead noted another deplorable aspect of the existing situation: Because marijuana is considered a narcotic, there is a false connection in the eyes of some young people between marijuana and true narcotic drugs. This connection must be broken. Other sociologists would argue that heroin and other narcotics are seen by youths as an evil that far exceeds the parental disapproval involved in marijuana.

It is an undeniable fact that in their quest for marijuana young people are increasingly becoming exposed to the criminal elements of society. Several recent reports indicate that organized crime is moving into the marijuana traffic, due to the growing size of this lucrative market and the difficulty that amateurs have in satisfying demand because of such crackdown devices as Operation Intercept. To illustrate how profitable this market is, in the last week of December, 1969, two private pilots in a rented plane were apprehended with one ton of marijuana which they were trying to import into this country from Mexico. They paid $5,000 for that ton of grass, which at retail would be worth nearly half a million dollars, quite a markup by anyone's standards. Once the contact with the underground is made, young people can be lured into trying addictive drugs. This deplorable situation must be stopped.

152 INSTEAD OF REVOLUTION

These three problems, the widening gap between generations, the disrespect for all law, and the contact with criminal elements, all indicate that something must be changed.

THE ALTERNATIVES

The present situation with regard to marijuana use and the law is unacceptable. The alternatives offer no simple solution. There is no pat answer, and the best solution requires careful consideration of the trade-offs involved. As a nation we are deservedly frightened about the prospect of widespread drug use. It cannot be proved that marijuana use will sap the initiative that has moved the nation to where it is today, but throughout history people have been suspicious about the dangers of drug-induced euphoria. Marijuana may not even be as dangerous to society as alcohol—in fact, cool, logical assessment suggests that it isn't—but it may be half as dangerous or one-fourth as dangerous, and that must make us pause before we put any stamp of approval on it.

Just as we must make laws that will operate in the best interest of society, so must we also be vigilant to promote respect for law. With 10 to 12 million felons flagrantly violating marijuana laws, and with widespread feeling that these laws are unrealistic and unjust, we have a problem that far exceeds the question of law. Some who smoke marijuana may feel morally culpable in doing so, but an overwhelming majority do not feel that way and are resentful of the legal system that has made them lawbreakers.

The problems inherent in this situation are aggravated by the fact that most of these lawbreakers are part of a group that already feels alienated from the mainstream of American life. It is most tragic of all when we consider that it is the younger generation which finds itself living outside the law. These same young people soon will be given the task of making and enforcing our laws. And yet today they are committing crimes against society, crimes for which a great many of them have been given stiff punishment, crimes which in their eyes are not wrong at all. It is a difficult problem.

This is the most critical trade-off, protecting society from the possibly dangerous effects of marijuana versus strengthening the walls that bar an important element of society from the mainstream. There are other trade-offs, such as stopping drug addiction at the first step of the parade of horribles versus destroying a great source of income for organized crime by making marijuana accessible through legal channels.

One other point must be brought up, and that is whether or not laws should be created to impose a morality on a society. If it can be shown that marijuana does not cause the user to behave in an antisocial manner, and that whatever damage it does is only to the individual involved, then can a logical case be made to prevent him from endangering himself if he so chooses?

The alternatives with which we have to deal in the marijuana question are:

1. Continue to consider marijuana sale, possession, and use a felonious act and seek, through an all-out campaign, to stop its widespread use.

2. Demote use and possession of marijuana to a misdemeanor, but continue to make the sale of marijuana or possession of more than a minimal amount a felony.

3. Make possession of less than two ounces of marijuana legal, but continue the harsh penalties for stockpiling or selling.

4. Make marijuana use legal and regulate the sale just as the sale of alcohol is regulated on the basis of purchaser's age and alcoholic content.

Two of these alternatives are untenable and can be quickly eliminated from consideration. It is clear beyond the shadow of a doubt that the first alternative is unacceptable. The existing situation, making mere possession a felony with harsher penalties than for possession of mescaline or such crimes as manslaughter, is ridiculous. We have all seen the damage that this law has wrought on the lives of many young people, none of them criminals except to the extent that we have branded them. The third alternative is also unacceptable, although many thoughtful people have endorsed it. If we feel as a nation that marijuana use should be made legal, then it seems clear that we should not subject the user to dealing with criminal elements in order to accomplish his legal desires. This illogical solution would only compound the lack of respect that young people hold for law in general.

We therefore have to choose between a modification of the

present crackdown on marijuana use and the acceptance of marijuana smoking on a par with the consumption of alcoholic beverages—the second and fourth alternatives. With all factors weighed in the balance, the best alternative seems to be legalization. The war against marijuana has been lost, and its use will continue to proliferate whether or not it is legalized. It cannot be shown that marijuana induces antisocial behavior to anywhere near the degree that alcohol induces behavior such as public drunkenness, violence, criminal acts, and automobile accidents causing thousands of deaths yearly.

Our greatest fear is that children high school age and younger simply are not mature enough to cope with marijuana, and we would like to see traffic in drugs eliminated or at least controlled. We have seen junior-high-school students standing in the schoolyard peddling drugs to their classmates and we know that access is not a problem, and may never be a problem again. We are not so much worried about the use of marijuana by these adolescents as we are worried about their possible progression to dangerous, hard drugs, which can cause permanent impairment. We recognize the trade-off between the possibility that legalization will increase accessibility, and the clear distinction that would thereafter be made between marijuana and the more dangerous drugs. Progression from marijuana to heroin or LSD or speed might be thwarted.

By regulating the use and sale of marijuana, the link between the marijuana user and the criminal elements dispensing it would be broken, and it is very likely that control of the illegal traffic in other drugs might be more possible.

How would the legal sale and distribution of marijuana be regulated? There are probably tobacco executives who dream of "Acapulco Gold" or "Panama Red" sold out of vending machines at every corner lunch counter. But the best course would be strict control of the sale, with behind-the-counter, unadvertised sales in such retail establishments as drugstores or liquor stores. Marijuana sale could involve procedures similar to those used in the sale of birth-control devices.

There must be strict penalties for the sale of marijuana to minors, just as there are strict penalties for the sale of alcohol.

No advertising of marijuana products would be allowed. The sale or acquisition of marijuana for those under the legal age would be a crime of the same magnitude (but not of greater magnitude) as the acquisition or sale of liquor for minors.

To settle the legal technicalities, the federal government should draft a model state law to cover all aspects of marijuana sale and use, such as the maximum legal dose (in terms of percentage of the active substance "T.H.C."), age limitations, method of sale, and penalties for violation.

Drug use among young people is a terrible problem which we must face head-on, but its greater significance is as a symptom of far more serious problems—disrespect for law, alienation of the young, the need of many for drug experiences—problems that could endanger our whole civilization. Here President Nixon has correctly identified the solution as one of education: education of the young, of their parents, and of the authorities. We may wish marijuana had never been discovered, but even if it had not, we would still have to face up to challenges issued by the new generation. It is manifestly clear that young people today are remarkably different from their predecessors, and their differences present rare opportunities for the cultivation of a better society and a better way of life for all people.

Chapter 13

INTERNATIONALISM

A New Voice in the World

Ever since the founding of the United Nations at the close of World War II, the destiny of America has been inexorably tied to events around the world. In trade, in travel, in military affairs, in communications bounced off satellites, the horizons of this country stretch far beyond its physical geography.

America's young have been influenced by these ties; no previous generation has been so engaged with the rest of the world. This is due in part to television, radio, newspapers, and film, but also in large part to expanding education. In unprecedented numbers young Americans are learning history and foreign affairs in high school and college. Moreover, they have grown up under the shadow of nuclear weaponry, which automatically internationalizes their concerns.

What have been the effects of the contact of America's young with their contemporaries around the world? How can our foreign policy best cope with these effects? What are the implications for the culture and the self-awareness of the young?

SOURCES OF CONTACT

The number of young Americans traveling abroad is vast. Many of this generation have been sent to war in Southeast Asia and others on police actions to Latin America, and a million of them, even in "peacetime," are at any moment stationed at military bases in Europe, Japan, and a score of other nations. Peace Corpsmen can be found in fifty-seven countries, and dozens of private organizations such as the American Field Service and the Experiment in International Living send students to live with foreign families throughout the non-Communist world. Other thousands of students study and travel independently. A good many students have befriended foreign youth studying here. This fellowship of young Americans and foreigners has quickened youth's interest in the customs and tastes of others.

Youth has seen the brutal statistics personified: a world one-third prosperous and two-thirds deprived, where 94 percent of non-Americans live on one-half the world's income, 80 percent in what we would call substandard housing, and 50 percent without minimally adequate diets. No one who has tried to find educated persons to lead literacy projects in an underdeveloped country (one-half of one percent of the rest of the world have a college education), no one who has seen the pathetic demonstrations for democracy in Greece or Argentina or who has tried to find a drink of pure water in an Indian village, can retain his confidence in the simplistic optimism that has informed the American view of the world. And one begins to discover that the American influence abroad is not the uniquely benevolent force that civics teachers say it is, that the underdeveloped world has often learned from us only the worst of American commercialism and materialism, not a love for democratic institutions and an equable distribution of wealth.

The complaints that foreign aid (the exiguous, string-wrapped $2 billion we now give) is bleeding the United States dry seem not only ignorant but callous. It is said that we cannot afford more foreign aid or lowered trade barriers for the underdeveloped nations; but we are told we can afford $30 billion a year for the Vietnam war in order to maintain an international image as an enemy of oppression. American youth traveling in other countries become skeptical of the rationalizations of American involvement that they heard at home—"peace-keeping operations," "protection against aggressors," and the like. They are embarrassed by their country more often than they embarrass it.

"The generation for which I speak has seen enough of warmongers," said John F. Kennedy. "Let our great role in history be that of peacemakers." The Peace Corps was established as an earnest of America's concern for the world's poor. Today, however, the Corps is under attack from many of its volunteers for alleged bureaucratization and overstaffing, for its failure to involve natives of host countries in administrative decision-making, and for its general willingness to sacrifice true effectiveness for prestige products that will make the program look good back home.

BRINGING US TOGETHER

This American generation reaching power can push forward an educational revolution around the world. For example, we might establish universities abroad to train teachers and other vitally needed professionals. Currently thousands of youth from developing nations are sent to the United States and other Western countries for advanced training and are tempted by superior job opportunities to stay after graduation; in fact, according to the Immigration and Naturalization Service, fully 30 percent do. The resulting brain drain thus counters the purpose of such programs. A first step in helping other nations keep their brightest talent would be to create college and technical facilities in the overseas nations themselves—on a no-strings basis—and by helping them finance adequate research and other sophisticated facilities to encourage the talented young to stay in their own countries after being educated.

Another educational tool American youth can put in the hands of the developing nations is the mass media. Most countries already have radio stations, and many have television. The United States Information Service (USIS) does provide some assistance, but the help could be greatly expanded. Specifically, the United States could aid nations in building whole television networks and educational systems such as we already have in Samoa.

One of the great failings of our own country is that we do not have a nationwide hostel system for youth from other lands. Surely our government, always eager to attract tourists and to encourage Americans to "see America first," should consider ways to develop such a system of inexpensive accommodations. Church groups, service organizations, universities, and chambers of commerce might work together for this purpose.

In the field of overseas service, America should take the lead in organizing an International Peace Corps, probably under the aegis of the United Nations. The objective would be to bring together the educated youth of industrial nations, join them with the Third World's elite youth, and direct all of them in peaceful construction of a better world. This personal contact through service would do more than any aid program to unite the world in common growth and purpose.

Under this proposal, the International Peace Corps organization would act chiefly as a clearinghouse for matching youth and service positions. The applicants and the various institutions in participating nations—rather than governments—would be connected directly. Hiring and work-living agreements also would be reached directly between the applicant and the given institutions abroad. The IPC would retain no in-country staff, and the volunteers' salaries would be paid by the host institution, an important psychological point, with reimbursement from the International Peace Corps. However, individual governments might decide to provide workers from their countries with certain services, such as medical care.

International Peace Corps volunteers would be trained in a specially established IPC school in the language and culture of the host country and, where necessary, would receive physical-fitness training. But volunteers would not be subject to any restrictions from the IPC. Their arrangements regarding travel, possession of an automobile (long a sticky problem in the U.S. Peace Corps), or the right to wear a beard would be made directly with the host institution. They also would agree to abide by local laws and respect local customs.

SCANDAL AND RENEWAL

Disillusionment marred another international youth effort when in 1967 the NSA-CIA scandal broke. The National Student Association had been founded after World War II as a voice for American college and graduate students; it served as a means of sharing common campus-government techniques and also as an agency of communication and solidarity with students in other countries.

During the cold war the CIA looked to the student group as a mechanism for influencing student opinion around the world. Since America was in the throes of McCarthyism at the time and the NSA had a somewhat liberal tinge, Congress could not be expected to approve support, the State Department felt similarly constrained, and the job fell to the CIA.

In return for their support, the CIA insisted on approving the leadership of the national body before it was elected and occasionally laid down other stipulations, such as a watered-down Vietnam statement at one of the NSA congresses. It all came out eventually when an NSA official leaked the whole story to *Ramparts* magazine.

The NSA-CIA scandal represented a moral dilemma whose proper response only became clear to the student participants after the scandal broke: better no foreign programs at all rather than one secretly backed by an intelligence agency. But the most telling lesson of the episode was the government's indifference to the right of young people to exercise independence of moral judgment. After the scandal the administration blithely appointed a committee headed by Secretary of State Dean Rusk to find a new formula for subsidizing the "CIA orphans." Most of the committee's ideas involved some sort of subsidy openly given without strings, as if that were possible. But no decision was made.

In such a fashion was a legitimate and important world role of American youth compromised and then abandoned. Today the NSA is not much interested in overseas activity. The pendulum of concern has swung to the student-power issues at home. But meanwhile American youth have lost a leadership role in the world, surrendering initiative to the Soviet Union, which is propagating anti-American feeling, particularly among the socialist youth of Scandinavia and southern Europe.

The administration should give fresh consideration to revising all the current and recently cut-back international exchange programs involving youth, including the "CIA orphans." While youth leadership properly may be directed toward student-power issues at home, it must also become engaged in speaking for American youth abroad and in getting to know its counterparts overseas. The kind of official exchanges enjoyed in the past should be re-evaluated. The old formal tour may be outdated. Programs in which American youth can actually work and live with their foreign counterparts would be more useful. If the future leaders of the community of nations are to understand each other, they must come to know each other, and the earlier the better.

New forms of financing are also needed. The widest possible interchange between youth leaders in America and those overseas should be encouraged by the government. However, the most propitious means for financing such a program would be for the President to appoint a group of American business, professional, and union leaders to raise the needed money privately. A fund-raising campaign blessed by the President probably would have success where current efforts are inadequate. If contributions were made tax-deductible, youth groups themselves could raise much of the needed funds.

An International Constituency

The youth of the United States and those of the Third World face radically different challenges. Most Third World nations have yet to acquire the material abundance that most of us take for granted (and have found inadequate as an end in itself). Therefore the communion of American youth is generally with the youth of the industrialized nations and the elite youth of the Third World who are wealthy enough to be concerned with higher education and political and social movements.

Several factors unite the youth around the world. First of all, prosperity (either among the masses or in select groups) has created whole classes of people who can afford to have a youth—a period clearly set apart from adolescence and full adult obligations when one is free to engage in idealistic causes and personal intellectual growth.

Second, youth all over the world are faced with rapid change. As the rate of change accelerates, respect for tradition and constituted authority is likely to be questioned. Especially when the society is marked by closed political channels or overbearing technology and bureaucracy, the young are likely to rebel.

The third catalyst that has inspired a truly worldwide youth consciousness is mass communications, which spread the youth culture all over the globe. For years America exported her young people's culture, but in the early 1960s Britain struck back with the Beatles, the Rolling Stones, and mod fashions (including long hair and unisex). Films from abroad—*Stolen Kisses, A Taste of Honey, Closely Watched Trains*—rival our own *Rebel Without a Cause* and *Easy Rider* as expressions of the special problems of youth. And from Canada came performers and composers like Ian and Sylvia, Joni Mitchell, and Leonard Cohen to enrich our folk-music scene and our poetry. We sent Bob Dylan to Britain, and they returned the favor with Donovan.

Moreover, each and every one of the issues discussed in this book has its equivalent in a variety of other nations. Campus revolt? The Sorbonne, the London School of Economics, and the Latin American nations have had their share. Reform of the military? It has been a hot issue in West Germany. The voting age? All over the world, even in Communist states where the vote is meaningless, eighteen-year-olds have the franchise. Long hair? It was one of the first things banned by the tyrannical regime in Athens.

As in the United States, youthful activism around the globe has had an immense impact on the political scene:

Latin American revolutions often begin on the campus.

Young Soviet Jews are protesting their oppressed state to an extent their parents never considered.

The Paris riots of 1968 helped to terminate, eventually, the political career of Charles de Gaulle.

The tragic rebellions in East Germany and Hungary in 1956 and Czechoslovakia in 1968 were in large part the work of discontented young people.

In 1968, Yugoslavia's President Tito acquiesced to student demands rather than face possible revolt among his people.

The Red Guard in China represented one rather unsavory example of politicized youth, and acted as an expression of Chairman Mao's wishes.

In Japan, young people have for years been a potent force on the left, even forcing President Eisenhower to cancel a visit in 1960. In the 1969 elections to the house of representatives, a large number of young candidates were elected, reducing the average age of representatives from fifty-five to forty-five!

In Hungary, a "new left" movement idolizes Che Guevara, to the annoyance of older, more doctrinaire Communists.

Even the youthful conservative movement is worldwide: A group calling itself the Movimento Europa Civilta, based in Italy, stages political "happenings" in Eastern Europe, distributes anti-Communist leaflets, and provides a source of great irritation to officialdom.

We could go on and on with examples of how young people in many nations have participated in the political process and created a genuine impact on their nations' destinies. Suffice it to remark that in one year, 1968, young people threatened or even terminated the careers of such powerful men as de Gaulle, Tito, and Lyndon Johnson. The youth constituency has arisen, and national leaders can ignore it only at their peril.

Perhaps the ultimate reason for the protests of young people is that they have always been called upon to obey the rules of society —become educated, take their places in the economy, and above all, offer their lives in time of war—yet are denied an active role in the decisions that shape their future. Now they are refusing to remain powerless.

And so America's youth phenomenon is part of a larger, global movement by those who, better educated, better informed, and more responsible than any previous generation, demand rights appropriate to their abilities. Only if older Americans, and older people in other lands, see these demands as opportunities for making the best use of young talent, and not as threats, will the nation and the world successfully weather the storm. That is all, really, that the "youth rebellion" wants.

EPILOGUE

This book on youth, like past Ripon efforts on other subjects, has a history in political action that parallels its substantive proposals. The book was begun in early 1969 as a report to the President on youth. Entitled "Bring Us Together," it suggested some sixty concrete measures by which Mr. Nixon might set a national climate conducive to a reconciliation between the generations. It was given preliminary approval at a meeting of The Ripon Society's National Governing Board in April, 1969, and was published in the September, 1969, issue of the *Ripon Forum*.

On December 16, 1969, six representatives of The Ripon Society met with President Nixon to discuss the report. The meeting was arranged by Senator Howard Baker, Jr., who accompanied the Ripon representatives into what was originally scheduled as a fifteen-minute session with the President and two of his aides. The dialogue with Mr. Nixon lasted fifty minutes and covered the following points:

1. *The substance of the report itself.* The President discussed with Bruce K. Chapman, the editor of the report, a number of the specific suggestions contained in it. He expressed agreement with Ripon's program for a volunteer army, which he said had influenced his own thinking when the program was first issued in 1967. He expressed concern for new measures to improve university quality. Education in this country, he said, was run by a "hidebound educational establishment" that impeded innovation.

2. *The communications problem with the young.* Ripon representatives told the President that he had a two-way communications problem with young people. His message was not getting out, and their message was not getting in. Those Presidential proposals that had intrinsic appeal to young people—the volunteer army, a U.N.-sponsored voluntary action corps, an extension of the White House Fellows program to state and local government—were not well known on college campuses. The President had the programs to deliver a youth message to Congress if he would only use them. The concerns of young people were not being voiced directly to the

President, the Ripon representatives pointed out. Despite his campaign pledge of an "open presidency," this meeting with Ripon was the first of its kind in the Nixon Administration. Ripon proposed that the President have more such meetings, that he consider setting up a youth advisory council, and that he plan televised sessions in which he would answer the questions of young people. The President said that the latter suggestion was already under serious consideration.

3. *Getting the input of youth.* The President designated Leonard C. Garment, his special assistant, to work with Ripon in developing a program to involve young people to a greater extent in government. He specifically approved the concept of task forces to report to him in selected areas of policy and to wed the freewheeling investigative techniques of Nader's Raiders with The Ripon Society's experience in developing concrete proposals. He expressed a desire to review personally the plans for such task forces to assure maximum impact. He said that the input of youth should not be limited to "youth issues" only.

4. *The problem of bigness.* The President cited this as the root of the youth revolt. Vietnam, he said, was a symptom rather than a cause of youth unrest. He quoted a French visitor who recently told him, "Your problem is war; ours is peace." Youthful unrest, President Nixon said, exists in all highly developed societies. He attributed it in part to the problem of modern bureaucracy—not only in government but also in the private and volunteer sectors. The young people come into institutions "bright-eyed and bushy-tailed" and eager to serve, he said, but in a few years they become frustrated. He cited the problem of bureaucracy and involvement as a major one for American society. The inability to make an impact in complex organizations creates demoralizing conditions in the federal government and elsewhere.

5. *Legislative measures.* Though Eugene Cowan, Special Assistant for Legislative Affairs, was in attendance, no Presidential follow-up was agreed to on Ripon recommendations for an omnibus youth bill and a Presidential message to Congress on youth.

The Ripon Society followed up on the President's interest in adapting Ralph Nader's techniques with a proposal for Open Presidency Task Forces that would be run from the White House. Each task force would be composed of four or five students; the administration would designate a high-ranking official to see to it that each group received the information it needed. Task forces would also work with senior advisers to assure some seasoned guidance, but neither these advisers nor the administration contacts would assume any control over the groups' work products, which might be written reports, confidential memos, or even films. The Ripon Society, after some consultation with student leaders and members of the President's Advisory Council on Executive Organization (the Ash Council), submitted a list of ten topics for task-force activity.

The President reacted favorably to the proposal but suggested that White House administration of the program might compromise its independence. Ripon accordingly moved to set up an independent, nonprofit, nonpartisan foundation to run the program and made tentative arrangements for a major fund-raising banquet in Dallas in early April. A letter from the President endorsing the concept, expected in time for this event, was inexplicably delayed.

In late May, after the outpouring of student opinion in response to the Cambodian invasion and the Kent State killings, the letter of endorsement came. It was very generously worded. The President called the project "an exciting experiment in giving government the benefit of the fresh ideas and careful scrutiny of responsible young people." He pledged that his administration would "cooperate with the work of the task forces and give careful consideration to the final reports. But the task forces should also feel free to give their findings a wider audience as they see fit; for in investing in this experiment, I hope that we shall get not simply ideas of immediate use to the day-to-day operation of government, but controversial ideas whose time may be yet to come." The first task force—on bureaucratic and congressional obstacles to the creation of an all-volunteer army—has yet to report, and various legal and financial details of the program are still being settled. But it does seem that this experiment, in which The Ripon Society no longer has an official part, is launched on its own. It is constituted as a separate corporation—the Open Presidency Corporation—funded through the Sabre Foundation of Fond du Lac, Wisconsin.

It will operate on a modest scale and with a heavy input of volunteer effort, but it may help to pioneer new patterns of collaboration between the generations. It may provide a bridge of sorts between the world of politics and the world of ideas. It may give young people a way to have a real impact on policy.

Meanwhile, the report that started it all has now grown into this book—The Ripon Society's seventh since its founding in December, 1962. Like the others it is the work of many hands; like the others it has been done mostly by volunteers working long hours because they believe that their ideas can make a difference. And the experience of The Ripon Society can testify to the fact that ideas followed up by patient and often frustrating work within the American governmental system can indeed make a difference.

Named after Ripon, Wisconsin, the birthplace of the Republican party, The Ripon Society began with only seventeen members. It is still far from a mass organization, yet it has moved to change the tone of political debate in the eleven cities in which it now has chapters. It attempts to reach out to groups that have never considered voting Republican and to build bridges to the professional, academic, and business communities. It offers politicians research, political aid, and a monthly magazine, the *Ripon Forum,* with independent criticism and positive proposals. Its members adhere to the Republican party not for what it is but for what they can make it become. They are now working at the White House, in government agencies, and on political staffs at all levels of government, and some have run for office.

Ripon's mottoes have always been simple. Its members have sought not expedient slogans but "the ideas whose time is yet to come"; and many of their programs for welfare reform, a volunteer army, revenue sharing, and policy toward China and Vietnam have helped shape national policy. They have sought not heroes to admire but ways to galvanize themselves to action. As the society's first statement said: "This, then, is a call to action. . . . The question is often asked, Where are the leaders of the new Republican party? We have shown just how we need such men. If we cannot find them, let us become them."

This spirit of challenge will ultimately affect all of America's institutions, because it represents attitudes that are widely diffused among a generation of young people whose political behavior is "aristocratic" in the classical Greek sense: They seek a meaningful public role that is not directly related to their own pecuniary interest. They have a strong notion of service, of political participation, and of public—as opposed to private—good. They prefer to work in organizations in which they can feel themselves colleagues rather than subordinates. They have a strong distaste for hierarchical structures, and when subjected to them—in the church, in the university, in the army, or in government or corporate bureaucracy—they begin to press for reforms. They have a well-developed sense of privacy, of tolerance for dissent, and of individual freedom and responsibility. They are willing to devote portions of their lives to voluntary work and may even plan their careers in such a way as to give prominence to social concerns. They tend to choose as leaders not men with an authoritarian style but those who are able to enlist them in a spirit of partnership around projects that have immediate practical consequences but at the same time serve a higher and well-articulated vision. They tend to conceive of their lives as a process not of material accumulation nor even of bureaucratic advancement but of learning, adventure, and service.

America has always had aristocrats of this sort. Indeed, the republic was founded by such men, and the success of its democratic system has depended on them. They have usually been confined to one class, however. Now a whole generation has grown up under conditions conducive to the growth of public-spiritedness. They have not known the cataclysm of a depression or a world war, so they think of social problems as manageable. They have not known want, so they are not preoccupied with material security. They have been well and freely educated, so they demand convincing reasons for the rules they must obey. And they have had political models that convince them that politics need not be narrowly manipulative. From Eisenhower they saw that it could be decent; from Kennedy, that it could appear noble and exciting; from Martin Luther King, that it could be infused with religious commitment. And from Richard Nixon they may have also learned a vital lesson: the importance of tenacity. Their standards are high, and they will not compromise them for short-term advantage.

This description is often said to fit only a small, vocal group at a few elite universities, but those who so dismiss it are well behind the times. The new class is, in fact, a mass aristocracy. Its members can be found at schools in all regions of the country and also among young labor-union members and white-collar workers. They are in the U.S. Army and in the slums. There are some working in police departments and in businesses. They tend to predominate in the professions, but no matter what their field, independence of spirit and public concern, rather than occupational or educational status, are the hallmarks of the new aristocrats. Political engagement will assume new importance in American life, because they will insist on it.

The impact of their concerns is already evident, not only in pressures for reform in old institutions but also in the invention of new institutional forms. The public-interest lawyer, the Peace Corps volunteer, the community organizer, the environmental planner—these are a few of the roles that the new class has already created for itself. More innovation is bound to come: new kinds of communities and economic enterprises, new techniques for expanding the democratic process itself. These changes—like all innovations—will be pioneered on a small scale by local and private groups. Yet their chances of spreading will depend on the climate of national politics. The demands of this mass aristocracy on national politics will thus be revolutionary; they will attempt to open institutions to new surges of creativity and public-spiritedness, but the tactics for change should be moderate.

Moderates are best at intelligent discussion, at persuasion, at developing workable proposals. When they decide to cooperate with each other, they are able to pioneer new institutional forms, to forge patterns of collaboration between generations, and to achieve results. They are capable of exciting others with ideas and eliciting sustained commitment. If they lead from their strength—not mass demonstrations but reason, competence, persistence, and tough-minded idealism—they can revolutionize the political system.

The experience of The Ripon Society may give some hope for these quiet tactics.

Josiah Lee Auspitz
President, The Ripon Society
Cambridge, Massachusetts

NOTES

CHAPTER 2

1. Guy Debord, *La Société de Spectacle* (Paris: Buchet-Chastel, 1967).
2. Jules Henry, *Culture Against Man* (New York: Random House, 1963), p. 29.
3. R. D. Laing, *The Politics of Experience* (New York: Ballantine Books, 1967), p. 58.
4. Sigmund Freud, *Civilization and Its Discontents* (New York: Doubleday Anchor, 1930), p. 86, in a footnote on Franz Alexander's *Psychoanalyse der Gesamtpersonlichkeit*. The scope of this article limits me to merely sketching these arguments and leaves me open to misinterpretation at this point. I would not urge a return to an "old-fashioned morality" with strong father figures, a reactionary strategy only too easy (given the difficulty of developing progressive approaches to child rearing) for many of the young to adopt (along with a simple-minded rejection of technology and an incoherent nature mysticism). I would argue that (1) "the introjection of the super-ego," which Freud believed to be essential to the maintenance of civilization, is essential only to organization against scarcity and is a positive hindrance to the development of a peaceful, non-repressive, post-scarcity society; (2) because societies foster the development of character types which are necessary to maintain those societies, "permissiveness" is essential to produce people who will fit into our liberal capitalism, i.e., passive, guilt-ridden, ineffectual consumers (see Henry, *op. cit.*); but those mechanisms necessary for the perpetuation of bourgeois society also produce the negation of that society, i.e., the youthful "counter" culture; and (3) what we must develop is the communal rearing of children, the dissolution of sex-role distinctions, the affirmation and protection of infant and adolescent sexuality, and a non-manipulative, non-directive approach to education. See Laing, *op. cit.*, as well as Wilhelm Reich's *The Sexual Revolution*, A. S. Neill's *Summerhill*, and my article, "The End of History," in *Broadside and the Free Press*, Vol. 9, Issue 1.
5. Jack Kerouac, *On the Road* (New York: Signet Edition, 1955), p. 148. The section of *On the Road* from which I have excerpted this passage has always been particularly infuriating to liberals whether white (Norman Podhoretz in the Spring 1958 *Partisan Review*) or black (James Baldwin in *Nobody Knows My Name*). The black radical

Eldridge Cleaver, however, defends it in *Soul on Ice*. For another defense of Kerouac by a black radical, see Julius Lester in *Liberation*, December 1969.

6. Allen Ginsberg, *Howl and Other Poems* (San Francisco: City Lights Books, 1956), pp. 9, 17.

7. Lawrence Lipton, *The Holy Barbarians* (New York: Julian Messner, 1959), p. 308.

8. One of the most vocal and popular intellectuals in the service of power is Bruno Bettelheim. For a sample of his views that "they are sick" (repackaged for popular consumption in the mass media), see *The New York Times Magazine*, January 11, 1970.

9. See Tom Wolfe's *The Pump House Gang* (New York: Farrar, Straus & Giroux, Inc., 1968).

10. See Louis Kampf's article, "Notes Toward a Radical Culture," in Priscilla Long's *The New Left* (Boston: Porter Sargent, 1969).

11. *The All Time Million Seller Records, 1970 Edition* (Woodland Hills, Calif.: Phono-Graph Publications, 1969).

12. I have borrowed this term from Susan Sontag in the chapter "Happenings: An Art of Radical Juxtaposition" in her *Against Interpretation* (New York: Farrar, Straus & Giroux, Inc., 1966).

13. Problems with copyright prevent me from quoting rock music lyrics and thus obviate any detailed textual criticism.

14. Patrick Waldberg, *Surrealism* (New York: McGraw-Hill), p. 13.

15. Even if I were not working under space limitation, I'm not sure I'd care to add much more than these brief comments to the millions of words, most of them nonsense, that have been written about drugs in recent years. My very subjective recommendations for further reading on the subject: the best book on America's youthful drug culture, Tom Wolfe's *The Electric Kool-Aid Acid Test*, the best book on the drug experience, Carlos Casteneda's *The Teachings of Don Juan: A Yaqui Way of Knowledge*. Both are available in ubiquitous paperback editions.

16. Anthony Carthew, *The New York Times Magazine*, September 6, 1964.

17. *The New York Times*, December 15, 1964. Before it was over (Kores switched to a private school) this case would become a sufficiently hot news item to merit (December 22) a *Times* editorial.

18. *Newsweek*, February 14, 1966.

19. *Life,* June 21, 1968.

20. *The New York Times,* October 20, 1968.

21. *Time,* January 26, 1970. Between the lines of this article, in which the *Time* writers can barely contain their disgust with Gernreich, he emerges as a witty Dadaesque con man of the fashion world.

22. Isadore Barmash, *The New York Times,* March 2, 1969.

23. *Ibid.*

24. Hans Richter, *Dada: Art and Anti-Art* (New York: McGraw-Hill, 1965), p. 90.

25. Henry, *op. cit.,* p. 25.

26. *Ibid.,* p. 132.

27. *Ibid.*

28. *Ibid.*

29. *Ibid.,* p. 137.

30. Laing, *op. cit.*

31. Richter, *op. cit.,* p. 109.

CHAPTER 3

1. Urban Research Corporation, 5464 South Shore Drive, Chicago, Illinois 60615.

2. American Institute of Public Opinion, May 25, 1969.

3. *Newsweek,* March 10, 1969.

4. See, e.g., Hastings Rashdall, *The Universities of Europe in the Middle Ages* (Oxford: Clarendon Press).

5. Quoted by David Dempsey, "Bruno Bettelheim Is Dr. No," *The New York Times Magazine,* January 11, 1970.

6. Alfred North Whitehead, *The Aims of Education* (New York: Macmillan, 1929).

7. National Student Association, *Student Guide to Legal Rights.*

8. "Time Essay," *Time,* May 2, 1969.

9. *Atlantic Monthly,* April, 1969.

CHAPTER 4

1. Brendan Sexton, "Middle Class Workers and the New Politics," unpublished manuscript.

2. Pete Hamill, "The Revolt of the White Lower Middle Class," *New York* magazine, April 14, 1969.

3. Sexton, *op. cit.*

4. *The American Political Science Review,* December, 1969, pp. 1104–1105.

Chapter 5

1. *Better Living* magazine, November/December, 1969, p. 25.
2. *Fortune,* January 1969, p. 142.
3. "The Younger Generation: An RIA Survey of College Students."
4. *Fortune,* January, 1969, pp. 180–81.
5. *Ibid.,* p. 78.
6. Norman Mailer, *The Armies of the Night* (New York: Signet Books, 1968), pp. 103–104.
7. *Better Living* magazine, November/December, 1969, p. 31.
8. *The New York Times,* January 4, 1970.
9. *Better Living* magazine, November/December, 1969, p. 6.
10. *The New York Times,* December 22, 1969, p. 18.
11. *Ibid.,* November 19, 1969, p. 37.
12. *Ibid.,* December 22, 1969, p. 18.
13. *Ibid.,* December 20, 1969, p. 33.
14. *Ibid.,* January 11, 1970, p. 62; *Newsweek,* January 19, 1970, pp. 55–56.

Chapter 6

1. *The Ripon Forum,* December, 1966.
2. See, *e.g.,* Bruce K. Chapman, *Our Unfair and Obsolete Draft— and What We Can Do About It* (New York: Pocket Books, 1968), and Robert T. Stafford *et al., How To End the Draft: The Case For an All-Volunteer Army* (Washington, D.C.,: National Press, 1967).
3. *The Boston Globe,* January 26, 1970, p. 11.
4. *The Progressive,* January, 1970, p. 17.
5. *Congressional Record,* November 5, 1969.
6. *Joint Hearings Before the Subcommittee on Constitutional Rights of the Committee on the Judiciary and a Special Subcommittee of the Committee on Armed Services, United States Senate, Eighty-Ninth Congress, Second Session: Bills to Improve the Administration of Justice in the Armed Services: Part I* (to be cited as *Hearings*), p. 196.
7. The *New York Times Magazine,* February 22, 1970, p. 38.
8. *Hearings,* p. 167.
9. *Ibid.,* p. 54.
10. *Ibid.,* p. 55.
11. *Ibid.,* p. 55.
12. *Ibid.,* p. 57.
13. *Congressional Record,* November 5, 1969.

14. *Ibid.*
15. *Hearings,* p. 144.
16. *Ibid.,* p. 347.
17. *Ibid.,* p. 338.
18. *Ibid.,* p. 16.
19. *Ibid.,* p. 4.
20. *Ibid.,* p. 4.
21. *Ibid.,* p. 5.
22. *Congressional Record,* November 5, 1969.
23. *Hearings,* p. 158.
24. *Ibid.,* p. 159.
25. *Ibid.,* p. 167.
26. The *New York Times Magazine,* February 22, 1970, p. 40.

CHAPTER 8

1. *The New York Times,* May 25, 1969, p. 68.
2. *Boston Globe,* December 4, 1969, p. 21.
3. Jack Newfield, *A Prophetic Minority* (New York: Signet Books, 1967), p. 39.
4. *Ibid.,* p. 43.
5. *Ibid.*
6. Stokely Carmichael and Charles V. Hamilton, *Black Power: The Politics of Liberation in America* (New York: Vintage Books, 1967), pp. 92–93.
7. Jerome Skolnick, director, *The Politics of Protest* (New York: Clarion Books, 1969), pp. 30–31.
8. *Fortune,* January, 1969, p. 71
9. *The Presidential Nominating Conventions 1968* (Washington, D.C.: Congressional Quarterly Service, 1968), p. 178.
10. *The New York Times,* December 17, 1969.
11. *Ibid.,* November 12, 1969.
12. *National Review,* December 2, 1969, p. 1202.
13. *The New York Times,* December 14, 1969.
14. *The American Political Science Review,* December, 1969, p. 1104.
15. *Newsweek,* December 29, 1969.
16. *The New York Times,* December 21, 1969, p. 35.

CHAPTER 9

1. *The New York Times,* January 2, 1970.
2. Her Majesty's Stationery Office, London, July, 1967.

3. "Vote at 18? A Pro and Con Discussion," *Senior Scholastic,* September 17, 1952.

4. "The American Forum of the Air," January 31, 1954.

5. Youth Franchise Coalition.

6. *Congressional Record,* June 24, 1969.

7. *Congressional Digest,* 1954.

8. *Congressional Record,* June 24, 1969.

9. *Student Impact* magazine, December, 1968, p. 49.

10. *The New York Times,* December 7, 1969.

11. Louis Harris, nationally syndicated column, March 7, 1968.

CHAPTER 10

1. *Wall Street Journal,* November 28, 1969.

CHAPTER 12

1. *U. S. Tobacco Journal,* October 30, 1969, p. 4.

2. *Washington Post,* November 26, 1969, p. A-13.

3. E. R. Bloomquist, *Marijuana* (New York: Glencoe Press, 1968), p. 142.

4. *The New York Times,* September 18, 1969, p. 43.

5. *Newsweek,* July 24, 1967, p. 52.

6. James A. Foley and Robert K. Foley, *The College Scene: Students Tell It Like It Is* (New York: Cowles, 1969).

7. *The New York Times,* November 16, 1969, p. 42.

8. *Newsweek,* July 24, 1967, p. 48.

9. *The New York Times,* February 13, 1970, p. 15.

10. *Newsweek,* February 16, 1970, p. 65.

11. *Wall Street Journal,* December 16, 1969.

12. Joe-Hin Tijo, W. N. Pahnke, and A. A. Kurland, "LSD and Chromosomes," *Journal of the American Medical Association,* November 3, 1969.

13. See, e.g., Lester Grinspoon, "Marijuana," *Scientific American,* December, 1969; Andrew T. Weil, "Cannabis," *Science Journal,* September, 1969; Norman E. Zinberg and Andrew T. Weil, "Effects of Marijuana on Human Beings," *The New York Times Magazine,* May 11, 1969.

14. Joel Forte, "Pot, A Rational Approach," *Playboy,* October, 1969

15. Tonight (TV show), January 28, 1970.

ABOUT THE CONTRIBUTORS

HOWARD H. BAKER, JR., was elected in 1966 as the first Republican Senator from Tennessee in modern times and is one of the youngest members of the Senate. An attorney, he is a member of the Committees on Commerce and Public Works and the Select Committee on Small Business.

HOWARD L. REITER (Editor) is a doctoral candidate in political science at Harvard and has edited the *Ripon Forum*. He worked on the Rockefeller campaign in New York in 1966 and in the Office of the Secretary of Health, Education and Welfare in 1967 and 1968. His writing has appeared in several Ripon publications, *The Nation,* and *Blue Collar Blues* (edited by Sar A. Levitan).

*　　　　*　　　　*

RUSSELL EDGERTON (coauthor, Chapter 11) is Assistant to the Secretary of Health, Education and Welfare, concerned mainly with education policy. After receiving his doctorate at Columbia, he was assistant professor of political science at the University of Wisconsin. He is the author of a forthcoming study of executive policymaking in the foreign aid program.

MARC J. GLASS (Chapter 6), a graduate of Harvard College and the Harvard Law School, is associated with the law firm of Nathanson and Rudofsky in Boston. A member of Ripon's National Governing Board, he worked for the Community Legal Assistance Office in Cambridge, and is responsible for the major part of the military-law section of Chapter 6.

WILLIAM J. KILBERG (Chapter 4) is General Counsel for the Federal Mediation and Conciliation Service, having been a White House Fellow assisting former Secretary of Labor George P. Shultz. A graduate of Cornell and the Harvard Law School, he has been active in The Ripon Society and a contributor to the *Ripon Forum* and the *Harvard Journal on Legislation*.

MARTIN KRAMER (coauthor, Chapter 11) is a staff member of the Office of the Assistant Secretary of Planning and Evaluation at HEW. A graduate of Harvard and a former Rhodes scholar, he spent two years teaching philosophy at the University of Texas, and worked in the Bureau of the Budget and the National Institute of Mental Health.

KEITH MAILLARD (Chapter 2), who has run a rock-poetry-comment program over the Boston radio station WBUR, has had work published in local underground papers, *The Resistance* and *Broadside/Free Press*. Classifying his work "in the Anarchist tradition," he wishes to acknowledge the helpful comments of M. C. Smith, David Omar White, Sandi Mandeville, and Dave Wilson.

DAVID C. NIKLAUS (Chapter 7) is field representative for Representative Paul N. McCloskey, Jr. (R.-Calif.) in San Mateo, California. He was special assistant to former Senator Thomas H. Kuchel, of California, for three years and prior to that was dean of students at Tennyson High School near San Francisco.

FRANK D. RAINES (Chapter 3), a Harvard senior majoring in government, has been chairman of the Student-Faculty Advisory Council at Harvard and was a leader of the moderate strike group in April, 1969. He was a staff assistant to Daniel P. Moynihan in 1969 and a vice-chairman of the White House Conference on Children and Youth.

BINKLEY SHORTS (Chapters 5 and 12) is a graduate of Pomona College and the Harvard Business School. Now employed in the Boston financial community, he has been active in the Cambridge chapter of The Ripon Society.

INDEX

Nazi Party, 79
Neo-McCarthyism, 28
New Deal, 106
New Left, 27, 38, 39, 42, 107, 120
  politics of commitment, 104–106
New Right, 106–107
New York City Board of Education, 35
New York Lawyers' Association, 77
New York Times, The, 19, 20, 109
New York University, 50
Newfield, Jack, 97
Newman Centers, 39
Newport Festival, 18
Newsweek (magazine), 20, 46, 144, 146
Niklaus, David C., 177
Nineteen-year-old vote, 110
Nixon, Richard M., 47, 66, 81, 88, 90, 91,
      111, 128, 130–131, 146, 147, 164,
      165, 168
Noise pollution, 59
Non-Linear Systems Company, 50
North Carolina College, 127
Nuclear test-ban treaty (1963), 100

Obscenity, 62
  use of, 4
Obsolete Youth (Bettelheim), 30
O'Callahan v. Parker, 70
Oedipus complex, 27
Office of Economic Opportunity, 62
Ombudsman, 128
On the Road (Kerouac), 9, 17, 81
Open Presidency Corporation, 166
Open Presidency Task Forces proposal,
      165–166
Operation Intercept, 151

Pacific Grove community (California),
      84
Panama Red (marijuana), 154
Panty raids, 5
Paris riots of 1968, 162
Paston, D. George, 77
Patriotism, xiv, 2, 96, 101
Peace Corps, 55, 121, 126, 131, 137
  established, 157–158
Peace movement, 100–102
  climax and denouement, 102–104
  compared with civil-rights movement,
      101–102
  November Moratorium (1969), 100
  purpose of, 102

Pentony, DeVere E., 40
Peoples Architecture (organization), 85
Philadelphia Plan, 40
Planned cities, 61
Planned Parenthood Federation, 88
Playboy (magazine), 150
Police brutality, 103, 104
Politics of commitment, 93–108
  equal rights, 96–100
  future of, 107–108
  New Left, 104–106
  New Right, 106–107
  peace, 96–100
  rewards of involvement, 93–96
Poor People's March of 1968, 100
Population, environment and, 88–90
Population Bomb, The (Ehrlich), 88
Populism, 47
Port Huron Statement (Students for a
      Democratic Society), 106
Poverty, 98
Powerlessness, sense of, 7
President's Advisory Council on Execu-
      tive Organization, 166
Price, Philip, 33–34
Price-fixing scandals, 59, 63
Profit motive, decision-making and, 59–
      61
Progressive Labor Party, 24, 38–39
Project GOO (Get Oil Out), 91
Psychedelic drug experiences, 18–19
Public officials, accountability of, 63
Pynchon, Thomas, 13

Radical dissidents, 27
Raines, Frank D., 177
RAND Corporation, 137
Reagan, Ronald, 103
Rebel Without a Cause (motion pic-
      ture), 11, 162
Red Cross, 120
Red Guard, 16, 162
Reiter, Howard L., 176
"Report of the Committee on the Age
      of Majority" (Great Britain), 110
Research Institute of America, 54
Resistance (organization), 21
Ressler, Paul, 20–21
Richter, Hans, 21–22, 25
Ripon, Wisconsin, 167
Ripon Forum (publication), 164, 167
Ripon Society, The, 114, 123–124, 126,
      130–131, 164–169